Excel for the Mac® Hot Tips

Ron Person
Christopher Van Buren

Excel for the Mac Hot Tips

Copyright© 1993 by Que® Corporation

Library of Congress Catalog No.: 93-83023

ISBN: 1-56529-162-X

96   95   94   93   4   3   2   1

Interpretation of the printing code: the rightmost double-digit number is the year of the book's printing; the rightmost single-digit number, the number of the book's printing. For example, a printing code of 93-1 shows that the first printing of the book occurred in 1993.

This book is based on Microsoft Excel for the Macintosh, Version 4.0.

Credits

Publisher
Lloyd J. Short

Associate Publisher
Rick Ranucci

Operations Manager
Sheila Cunningham

Publishing Plan Manager
Thomas H. Bennett

Acquisitions Editor
Chris Katsaropoulos

Title Manager
Shelley O'Hara

Product Director
Kathie-Jo Arnoff

Production Editor
H. Leigh Davis

Editors
William A. Barton
Elsa M. Bell
Jane A. Cramer
J. Christopher Nelson
Anne Owen

Technical Editor
Joseph A. Bunder

Book Designer
Scott Cook

Production Team
Claudia Bell
Julie Brown
Jodie Cantwell
Paula Carroll
Laurie Casey
Michelle Cleary
Brook Farling
Heather Kaufman
Bob LaRoche
Linda Seifert
Sandra Shay

Indexer
Johnna VanHoose

Composed in Utopia and MCPdigital by Que Corporation

Acknowledgments

The tips in this book come from years of application development and training in Excel for our clients. But some of the best tips, tricks, and work-arounds seem to come from the synergy of multiple minds facing similar tasks. I'd like to thank two fellow Microsoft Consulting Partners, Reed Jacobson of Arlington, Washington, and Don Buchanon of Burbank, California, for our dinners, phone conversations, and projects we've worked on together.

—R.P.

I would like to thank Chris Katsaropoulos for managing this project, Kathie-Jo Arnoff for first-rate product development, and Leigh Davis for superb editing. Also, thanks to Matt Wagner at Waterside Productions for managing my career.

—C.V.B.

Trademarks

All terms mentioned in this book that are known to be trademarks or service marks have been appropriately capitalized. Que cannot attest to the accuracy of this information. Use of a term in this book should not be regarded as affecting the validity of any trademark or service mark.

Mac and Macintosh are registered trademarks of Apple Computer, Inc.

Microsoft Excel is a registered trademark of Microsoft Corporation.

About the Authors

Ron Person is one of the original Microsoft Consulting Partners, Microsoft's highest rating for Microsoft Excel and Word for Windows consultants. He has written more than 14 books for Que Corporation, including *Using Excel 4 for Windows, Special Edition; Using Windows 3.1, Special Edition; Using Word for Windows 2, Special Edition;* and was coauthor of *Using Access for Windows, Special Edition.* Ron is the principal consultant for Ron Person & Co, based in San Francisco. The company is one of the leading developers and trainers in Microsoft Excel.

Christopher Van Buren is a veteran computer-book author with a dozen titles to his credit, including *Using Excel 4 for the Mac, Special Edition;* and *Using 1-2-3 for the Mac,* both published by Que Corporation. Although Chris specializes in spreadsheets, he also has written about desktop publishing, graphics, operating systems, and integrated programs.

Table of Contents

Introduction

Whether you are a beginning or experienced Excel user, the shortcuts and powerful techniques presented in *Excel for the Mac Hot Tips* will help improve your proficiency. Here you will find information about the subtle program features you were too busy to read about in the documentation. You also will find undocumented secrets, tips, and proven advice.

Unlike some computer books, it is not necessary to read the chapters or tips in this book in any particular order. Each chapter includes tips for a particular feature or function of Excel. That is, all of the toolbar tips are located in the "Using Toolbars" chapter and the macros tips are conveniently located in the "Creating Macros" chapter.

 Watch in particular for tips identified by a "Hot" icon. These are the author's favorites, and they are bound to pique your interest. You can find a list of the favorites on the inside front and back covers of this book.

If you would like a comprehensive overview of Excel, pick up a copy of Que's *Using Excel 4 for the Mac, Special Edition*.

Book Conventions

Certain conventions are used in *Excel for the Mac Hot Tips* to help you understand the techniques and features described in the text. This section provides examples of these conventions.

The following table shows special formatting used in this book:

Format	Meaning
italic	Emphasized text and variables
boldface	Text that you type
`special typeface`	Words that appear on-screen or in a figure or menu command prompts

In most cases, keys are represented as they appear on the keyboard. On your keyboard, some key names may be spelled out or abbreviated differently than shown here.

Key combinations, such as Shift+Tab indicates that you press the Shift key and hold it down while you then press the Tab key. Other key combinations are performed in the same manner.

1

Working with Files

An understanding of ways to efficiently work with Microsoft Excel files can help you create your own startup worksheet, open multiple files at one time, or remove unused space from files. Following are some tips to help you manage files more efficiently.

Open any document automatically on startup

When Excel starts, it automatically opens any worksheet, macro, or chart if you put the worksheet, macro, or chart file in the Excel Startup folder, located in the System folder.

If you are using System 7, the Excel Startup folder is in the Preferences folder, which is inside the System folder (System:Preferences:Excel Startup). When you no longer want this file to open automatically, delete or remove it from the Excel Startup folder.

Caution: If you place alias files into the Excel Startup folder (System 7 only), the alias files will not behave like normal files—that is, Excel will not automatically open them upon startup.

Create templates that appear in the File New dialog box

Templates are files that act as patterns on which to base new worksheets, macro sheets, or charts. A worksheet or macro sheet template can contain styles, column widths, text, numbers, formulas, names, custom formats, and so on.

It may be a finished worksheet except for the data values that need to be entered. A chart template contains all the formatting and settings used for a chart, but it contains no data.

Templates have many advantages. In addition to saving a tremendous amount of work, templates automatically let you save the file without destroying the original template: saving the filled-in template stores a normal worksheet file, which will never overwrite a template file.

If you save a template in the Excel Startup directory (refer to preceding tip), it will automatically appear in the File New dialog box as a type of new worksheet you can open.

To create a worksheet, macro sheet, or chart template, create the worksheet, macro sheet, or chart that contains all the contents and formatting you want in the template.

To save the worksheet, macro sheet, or chart as a template, complete the following steps:

1. Choose the File Save As command.

2. In the File Name edit box, type the name by which you want to recognize the template.

3. Choose the Options button, then select Template from the File Format drop-down list.

4. Change to the Excel Startup folder in the System folder (or Preferences folder for System 7 users). Choose OK.

You can save templates to and open them from any folder, but templates in the Excel Startup folder appear in the File New dialog box. The next time you open the File New dialog box, your template's name appears.

Create a custom startup worksheet

 You can create your own startup worksheet with the styles, named ranges, formulas, display settings, and other settings that you use most frequently. In fact, with a custom startup worksheet, each new worksheet you open will contain your custom settings.

To create your own default startup or new worksheet, open a new or existing worksheet. Use the existing worksheet or modify the sheet so that it contains all the settings, text, numbers, formats, styles, and formulas you need. If, for example, your company uses standardized styles for certain cell formats, put those styles in the worksheet.

If you normally create worksheets with a specific footer or header, put those in the worksheet. Modify the worksheet exactly as you want it to appear when you start Excel or choose File New. You can remove or customize the header/footer, remove worksheet grid lines and other worksheet elements, create custom number formats, create custom styles, add commonly used range names, and choose a new default font for the worksheet.

Save your worksheet as a template in the Excel Startup folder. Refer to the preceding tips for specifics about the Startup folder and templates.

Start Excel without a worksheet

If you find yourself closing the startup worksheet to open a different worksheet each time you begin Excel, you may want to open Excel without any worksheet in view. This way, you don't have unwanted worksheets around when you first enter the program. You can't start Excel without a worksheet open, but you can achieve a similar result: you can make the startup worksheet invisible.

To make the startup worksheet invisible, perform the following steps:

1. Open a new, blank worksheet and use the Window Hide command to make the worksheet invisible.

2. Quit Excel with File Quit.

3. When asked, save the changes you made to the worksheet and store the worksheet in the Excel Startup folder. Make sure that there are no other startup worksheets in the Excel Startup folder.

   The next time you start Excel, a worksheet does not appear, but an invisible startup worksheet is actually open.

Use a macro to locate the Excel Startup folder

Chances are that the Excel Startup folder is in your System folder or in the Preferences folder in your System folder. However, you may have changed the startup folder to an alternative startup.

If you have trouble finding your current startup folder (or if documents in the startup folder are not opening automatically), use the following macro to locate your current startup folder:

```
A1:  STARTUP
A2:  =GET.WORKSPACE(23)
A3:  =RETURN()
```

Run this macro from any macro file, and then use the
Options Display command with the Formulas option un-
checked to view the result in cell A2 of the macro sheet.
The result in A2 tells you the location of the current
startup folder.

Open a previously opened file by
selecting its name from the File menu

Excel stores the names of the last four worksheets you
used in the File menu. To quickly return to one of these
files, select its name from the menu. These document
names remain in place even after you quit Excel. Each
time you open and close a file, that file's name is added
to the list, replacing one of the four currently listed.

Close all files at once

To close all the open files, hold down the Shift key as you
choose the File menu. The Close All command replaces
the Close command. Choose Close All to close all open
worksheets, macro sheets, and charts. You are prompted
to save files that have been changed after they were initially opened. The Global macro and add-in macros are
not closed.

Install the free add-ins that come
with Excel

Excel comes with many free add-in features that give you
extra powers not automatically in the program. These
features are offered as add-ins because they can be some-
what specific; in other words, not every Excel user will
want them all. Thus, you can add the ones you like.

Add-ins are located in the Macro Library folder that appears in your Excel folder. (If the Macro Library folder does not appear, you must return to the Installation program and add the Macro Library to your existing Excel setup.)

To install an add-in to Excel, use the Options Add-Ins command and choose the Add button to locate new add-ins. Open the Macro Library folder and then open the desired add-in. Its name will appear in the add-in list.

Save files using a timed reminder

Excel comes with many free add-in features, one of which is an AutoSave feature that reminds you to save your work. When you add the AutoSave feature, it appears in your normal Excel menu as the Options AutoSave command.

Choosing this command displays the AutoSave dialog box shown in figure 1.1. When AutoSave is on, a check mark appears next to the AutoSave command in the menu.

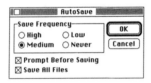

Fig. 1.1 *Use AutoSave to remind yourself to save your work.*

Send multiple files as a single document

Passing multiple Excel documents to another Excel user can be more convenient when all the documents are in a workbook. This precaution reduces the chance that you will forget a file. This technique also makes it easier to send files via electronic mail.

To bind documents into a workbook, perform the following steps:

1. Choose the File New command, select Workbook from the list, and choose OK.

   This action opens a blank workbook.

2. To bind documents into the workbook, click the Add button.

3. When the Add to Workbook dialog box appears, you can select an open document and bind it into the workbook by choosing the Add button.

4. To bind in an unopened document, choose the Open button and follow the same steps as if you were going to open the document.

   Bound documents appear as an icon of stacked pages on the workbook contents page. Bound documents exist only in the workbook. To send a workbook with a collection of files, make sure that the files are bound.

To remove a document from the workbook, select the file from the contents page and choose the Remove button. This is not the same as unbinding the worksheets.

Move quickly between workbook pages

To quickly move between workbook pages, press ⌘+Option as you click the mouse on any of the three page icons at the lower-right corner of a workbook document. The workbook shortcut menu displays the available documents. Click the document you want to activate.

Bind or unbind documents with a click

To bind or unbind documents from the workbook, switch to the workbook's content page. Click the icon at the right of the content page to toggle the document between bound and unbound. An icon represented as a stack of pages indicates a bound document.

The following icon shows a stack with loose pages and represents an unbound document:

Store summary information about a worksheet

You may be able to manage your worksheets better if you use the Document Summary add-in that is free with Excel. The Document Summary add-in invisibly stores summary information in the worksheet. It stores the date the sheet was created, the revision number, comments, and so on.

Storing the information in hidden names in the worksheet keeps the worksheet free from extraneous information. Figure 1.2 shows the document summary information for a typical worksheet.

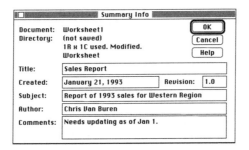

Fig. 1.2 *Use the Document Summary add-in to help manage document versions.*

To use the Summary Information feature, you must install the Document Summary add-in. Afterward, Document Summary add-in will be available when you run Excel.

To remove the Document Summary add-in, reopen the Add-In Manager, select the Document Summary add-in, and choose the Remove button.

To edit or review the summary information, choose the Edit Summary Info command. Edit the information in any of the edit boxes. You cannot change the creation date.

2

$$\boxed{\textsf{CHAPTER}}$$

Moving and Selecting

Although it's easy to move the active cell and select a cell or range, many tricks in Excel can make the process even easier or faster. In this chapter, you learn how to select a frequently used range with the press of a key and how to quickly move across large areas of the worksheet.

Some tips that save the most time are simple accessibility tips that make Excel quick and easy to use. And of course, everyone's favorite accessibility tip is how to use the shortcut menus.

Display shortcut menus

If you use a mouse, you will want to use one shortcut immediately—shortcut menus. Shortcut menus enable you to quickly access commands associated with the object on which you click.

For example, if you point to a cell and press the ⌘ and Option keys as you click the mouse button, a menu of commands related to modifying a cell displays. Pointing to a column (bar) in a chart and using the ⌘+Option+click technique displays a menu of commands related to modifying a column.

Shortcut menus appear underneath the pointer. Try clicking the following objects to access menu commands relating to the object:

Any cell
Row heading
Column heading
Any toolbar tool
Any object on the worksheet
Chart axis
Chart data series
Chart text
Chart plot area

Fill formulas or data into cells with Option+Return

 With this technique, you fill data or formulas in cells as you enter the data or formulas, saving the steps you normally need for the fill or copy and paste commands.

To fill data or formulas into selected cells or a selected range:

1. Select the cells or range you want to fill.

2. With the range still selected, enter the formula or data into the active cell within the selected range. The formula appears in the title bar.

3. Press Option+Return to enter the data or formula into each of the selected cells.

Numbers or text appear as constant values in each of the selected cells. Formulas are filled in each selected cell as though those formulas were filled with the Edit Fill Right/Down command or with the Edit Copy and Edit Paste commands. Relative references in formulas adjust to their new locations.

Move cells with drag-and-drop

With a mouse, you have many shortcuts available for rearranging your worksheet or macro sheet. One shortcut enables you to move a cell or range by dragging it to a new location and dropping it. This feature is known as *drag-and-drop.*

To drag a selected cell or range to a new location:

1. Select a single cell or a range that is a single block.

2. Move the pointer to the edge of the selected cell or range. When the cell pointer is correctly positioned over an edge of the selection, the pointer changes from the cross, normally seen over a cell, to an arrowhead pointer.

3. Hold down the mouse button and drag the cell or range to its new location. A shadowed outline of the cells being moved appears.

4. Release the mouse button to drop the cell or range at the new location.

Be careful that you do not position the pointer over the small square that appears at the lower right corner of a selection. This small square is used to fill cells by dragging.

If drag-and-drop is not working, select the Options Workspace command and place a check mark beside the Cell Drag-and-drop option; then click OK.

Copy cells with drag-and-drop

Copying a cell or range to a new location is as easy as dragging and dropping. Dragging and dropping copies of formulas creates copies the same as if you use Edit Copy and Edit Paste. When you fill in cells with drag-and-drop relative cell references, formulas adjust to their new locations.

To drag-and-drop a copy, follow the same procedure as the one just described for dragging cells to a new location. However, hold down the Control key as you drag the selection. As you hold down the Control key, a small plus (+) sign appears next to the pointer, indicating that you can make a duplicate. Drag the shadowed outline to where you want the copy, and then release the mouse button.

Fill formulas or data into cells by dragging the fill handle

When the drag-and-drop feature is turned on, a small square appears at the lower right corner of the cell or range selected. This square is the *fill handle*. You drag the fill handle to fill data or formulas into adjacent cells.

To fill a formula or data into adjacent cells:

1. Select the cell or range that contains the data or formula you want to copy.

2. Drag the fill handle in the direction you want filled. As you drag the handle, you see an outline surrounding the cells to be filled.

3. Release the mouse button to fill the cells.

Formulas are filled into cells the same as if you use Edit Fill Right/Down. Relative references in formulas adjust as they do with other types of copy or fill. You can drag in any direction—up, down, left, or right. You can fill only one direction at a time.

Erase cells with drag-and-drop

Drag-and-drop can help you erase all or part of a range of cells. The drag-and-drop feature must be turned on. Choose the Options Workspace command and select the Cell Drag-and-drop feature to turn on the drag-and-drop feature.

To erase all or part of a range of cells select the cells and then drag the fill handle up or left. Cells below or to the right of the dragged area appear patterned. When you release the mouse button all the patterned cells (those cells below and right) are erased. Figure 2.1 shows the direction to drag and the portions of the range erased when all months are selected and the fill handle is dragged to the left.

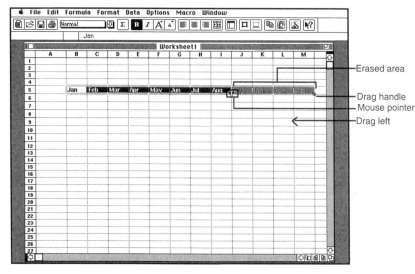

Fig. 2.1 *Drag the fill handle up or left to erase cells.*

To completely erase a range drag-and-drop, drag the fill handle up or left until the fill handle is over the top left cell in the original selection. Then release the mouse button.

Another way you can quickly blank cells with the drag-and-drop feature is by highlighting a block of empty cells in an unused part of the worksheet (preferably near the cells you want to erase). Now drag those blank cells onto the unwanted filled cells and release the mouse. Excel asks if you want to overwrite nonblank cells. Choose Yes to blank the entire destination area.

Return to one of your last four locations

When you use the Formula Goto command or the ⌘+G shortcut to move, Excel remembers the last four locations to which you moved. This capability enables you to go to a location, work there, and then return to your original location. To return to one of the last four locations, choose the Formula Goto command or press ⌘+G.

When the Goto dialog box displays, the last four cells or ranges you selected with Goto appear at the top of the Goto list. To return to that location, select one of these top locations and choose OK, or double-click the location in the list.

Use Goto to select a range with widely separated corners

It's tedious to select a large area by dragging across cells or using the Shift+arrow key combination. Instead, you can use the Goto dialog box command to make a large selection.

To make a large selection, follow these steps:

1. Select one corner of the large range.

2. Choose the Formula Goto command or press ⌘+G to display the Goto dialog box.

3. In the Reference edit box, type the reference for the opposite corner or a cell close to the opposite corner.

4. Hold down the Shift key as you choose OK or press Return. This action selects the entire range, from the original cell to the cell you typed.

If the cell you typed in step 3 is not the exact cell for the opposite corner, the range selected will not be the range you want. But you can adjust the current range to what you want. With the range selected, use the scroll bars to scroll to where you can see the cell you want as the opposite corner.

Hold down the Shift key as you click this new opposite corner. This action will select all the cells between the original cell and the cell on which you press Shift and click.

Use the Zoom view to select one or more large areas

The Zoom feature in Excel can also make it easy to select one or more large areas. If you reduce the size of the worksheet displayed in the window, you may be able to see and select all the large area you want to select. To reduce the worksheet in size so that you can see more of it, choose the Window Zoom command. From the Zoom dialog box, select 50% or 25% from the Magnification group, and then choose OK.

This action gives you an *aerial* view of the worksheet. Click one corner of the area you want to select, and then hold down the Shift key as you click the opposite corner. To select multiple areas, drag across the first area, and then hold down the ⌘ key as you drag across each additional area.

To return to a normal-sized worksheet, choose the Window Zoom command, select 100%, and then choose OK.

Move the active cell over a long distance with a double-click

Excel has an express move that enables you to move the active cell quickly across a block of cells that are either all filled or all empty. For this express technique to work, the *drag-and-drop* feature must be turned on, as described earlier in this chapter.

To move across a block of filled cells, as shown in figure 2.2, double-click the edge of the active cell on the side of the direction in which you want to move. In the figure, you would double-click the right edge of cell F7 to quickly move the active cell to cell H7. You can double-click any edge to make an express move in the direction of that side. The mouse pointer changes to the arrow head when correctly positioned over an edge.

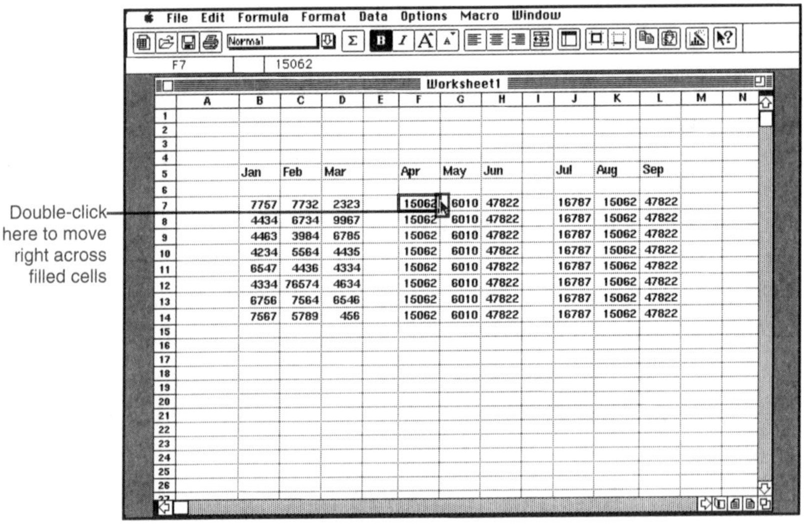

Double-click here to move right across filled cells

Fig. 2.2 *Move quickly across cells by double-clicking on an edge.*

If you start with a filled cell as the active cell, the express action moves the active cell over contiguous filled cells until reaching a blank cell. The selection stops on the last filled cell.

If you start with a blank cell as the active cell, the express action moves the active cell over contiguous blank cells until reaching a filled cell. The active cell stops on the last blank cell.

Select blocks of cells with Shift+double-click

You also can use the express move with the double-click just described to select the cells over which the active cell moves. To select cells over which the active cell moves, hold down the Shift key as you double-click the edge of a cell.

Select a large block of cells with Shift+Control+*(asterisk)

You will face many situations in which you need to select a large area of cells, such as a database, a report to print, or data to chart. If you correctly design the block of data you want to select, the selection process is easy—you can do it with a keystroke. This technique is also very useful for recorded macros that need to select a range that changes size.

In Excel, a *block* of cells is a group of cells that all touch edges or corners. This group of cells must be surrounded by the worksheet edge or blank cells. In effect, the block of cells must be an island not connected to other parts of the worksheet.

The following technique shows you how to select a block of cells with a single keystroke:

1. Select one cell in the block of cells that make up your database, report, or print area.

2. Press the Shift+Control+* (asterisk) key combination to select all touching cells. You also can use the Select Current Block tool in the Utility tools in the Customize dialog box. (Select Options Toolbars and choose Customize; then select the Utility tools.)

You also can use the macro recorder to record selecting an area with Shift+Control+*. When you run the macro, Excel selects the range just as if you pressed Shift+Control+*, even if the range changed size or shape.

The Shift+Control+* key combination offers a shortcut for choosing the Formula Select Special command and then selecting the Current Region option.

Insert rows, columns, or cells with Shift+Control++ (plus sign)

Inserting cells, rows, or columns is often the easiest way to rearrange your worksheet or create a new working area on a worksheet. Inserting works by moving the selected cells, rows, or columns down or to the right. New blank cells, rows, or columns are inserted at the location of the original selections.

Follow these steps:

1. Select the cells where you want new blank cells inserted.

2. Press Shift+Control++ (plus sign on typing keys).

3. Select from the Insert dialog box the direction you want existing cells to shift, and then choose OK.

When you insert rows or columns, Excel automatically moves cells down or to the right as appropriate.

Delete rows, columns, or cells with Control+- (minus sign)

Deleting and clearing cells, rows, or columns differ. When you delete, you pull the cells, rows, or columns from the sheet as though they never existed. Cells, rows, or columns from the right or below move in to fill the vacuum that remains.

Follow these steps:

1. Select the cells where you want existing cells deleted.

2. Press Shift+Control+- (hyphen on typing keys).

3. From the Insert dialog box, select the direction you want existing cells to shift to fill in the vacuum, and then choose OK.

When deleting rows or columns, Excel automatically moves cells up or to the left, as appropriate.

Insert or delete through multiple worksheets

To insert or delete the same cells, rows, or columns in more than one worksheet, use Excel's group edit feature. When group edit is enabled, the changes to one worksheet are duplicated in other worksheets in the group.

To make the same insertion or deletion in multiple worksheets, follow these steps:

1. Open all worksheets with which you want to work.

2. Activate the worksheet in which you want to make changes. Other worksheets will reflect the changes you make to this worksheet.

3. Choose the Options Group Edit command.

4. Select from the Select Group list the worksheets you want to be in the group.

   To select a contiguous list of worksheets, click the highest worksheet you want in the group and hold down Shift as you click the lowest. All worksheet names between and including these two are selected.

   To select a noncontiguous list of worksheets, click the first worksheet, and then use ⌘+click to click other worksheets you want in the group.

5. Insert or delete cells, rows, or columns through the active worksheet.

Changes you make to the active worksheet will be made to other worksheets in the group. All worksheets in the group appear with [Group] in their titles. To get out of group mode, activate one of the other worksheets in the group.

Check a cell's contents while preserving the selection

If you are checking formulas or errors in a worksheet, you may want to select an area and then check the contents of each cell in the area without losing your selection. This happens, for example, if you use the Formula Select Special command to select the cells containing errors.

To see the formula causing an error, you must click the cell, losing the selection of other cells that remain to be checked. You can, however, move through contiguous or noncontiguous selections and check or edit each cell while retaining the selection.

To keep all the cells selected, and to be able to see each of their contents in the formula bar, press the Tab or Shift+Tab key to move between the cells. When you find a cell you want to edit, press ⌘+U or click in the formula bar. After you finish editing, press Tab or Shift+Tab to move to the next cell in the selection.

Display the active cell in a large selection

If you scroll in the worksheet so that you can no longer see the active cell, but you want to move the active cell back into the portion of the window you can see, press ⌘+Backspace.

Select only blank cells

In a worksheet, you may have areas that have not yet been filled out. When you are ready to enter this data, you may find it useful to quickly highlight all blank cells in the active area of the worksheet.

Follow these steps:

1. Press ⌘+End to move to the high cell, the most remote corner of the worksheet—or the cell that marks the last row and column used in the worksheet.

2. Press Shift+⌘+Home to highlight from the high cell to cell A1. You have now highlighted the active worksheet area.

3. Choose the Formula-Select Special command.

4. Choose the Blanks option and press Return.

You now have highlighted all blank cells in the active portion of the worksheet. You can highlight blank cells in any selected range by dragging to highlight the range before you use the Formula-Select Special command.

Use your own names on frequently used ranges

 After you learn how to name areas of your worksheet with your own names, you can select areas with the press of a key. The areas even expand or contract if rows or columns are inserted or deleted through the original range, meaning that the names still refer to the correct range, even if you insert or delete cells, ranges, rows, or columns.

To assign a name to a cell or range:

1. Select the cell or range of cells you want to refer to by name.

2. Choose the Formula Define Name command. The Define Name dialog box displays.

3. Select the Name edit box and type in the name you will use to refer to the selected cell or range.

   Names use letters, numbers, underscores, or periods of up to 255 characters. Never use a space. Although you can use some symbols, you can't use many others.

4. Choose OK.

5. Save your worksheet or macro sheet if you want to save the name for the next time you open this file.

Now that the name is assigned to this range, you can select the range at any time by choosing Formula Goto (or pressing the Goto key, F5), selecting the name from the list, and choosing OK. (Choosing the F5 key is the same as choosing the Formula Goto command or the ⌘+G shortcut.)

Create a "data entry" range

 Your worksheet includes a data entry area with several cells that must be filled out, you can quickly highlight those cells and move among them by including them in a named range.

Use the following steps:

1. Highlight all the data entry cells.

2. Use the Formula Define Name command to assign the name Data Entry to the range.

3. You then can highlight and begin to fill out the range by using the (Goto) command or ⌘+G and jumping to the Data Entry range name in the Goto list.

4. Use the Tab key to move between cells in the highlighted data entry range.

3

Using Toolbars

In Excel 4.0, toolbars can save you considerable time. With toolbars, you can quickly reach commands you use frequently. You can even add your own macros to custom tools that you design. Some of these tools hold hidden surprises. This chapter offers some interesting toolbar tips.

Display the toolbar by using the shortcut menu

If you have a toolbar displayed in your worksheet, you can easily reach toolbar commands—click a displayed toolbar as you press the ⌘ and Option keys. This action displays the Toolbar shortcut menu shown in figure 3.1. The toolbar shortcut menu appears. Drag down to the name of the toolbar you want to display or hide, and then release the button.

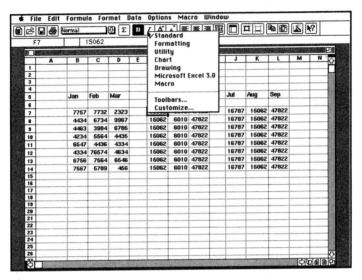

Fig. 3.1 *Click the toolbar while pressing ⌘+Option to display the list of other toolbars.*

View the names of tools on the toolbar

There are so many tools—it's easy to forget what they do. You can see what a tool does in two ways. First, you can click and hold onto a tool. As you hold down the mouse button, a description of the tool appears in the Status bar at the bottom of the screen. If you do not want to choose the tool's command, drag the tool onto the worksheet before you release the mouse button.

Second, you can browse through tool descriptions or receive help on a tool. Click the Help tool at the far right side of the Standard toolbar. The Help tool has the drawing of an arrow pointer and a question mark. (Press the Esc key to return to a normal pointer.)

After you click the Help tool, you can point to any tool (but don't click) on any toolbar and see its description in the Status bar at the bottom of the screen. If you click a tool, the Help window for that tool displays.

Use the alternate toolbar commands

Some tools in the toolbar offer an alternate action. To produce the tool's alternate action, hold down the Shift key as you click the tool. As you hold the Shift key and click a tool, you will see the tool's face change to reflect the Shifted action.

If you don't know what will happen when you hold down the Shift key, you can see what the tool does by holding down the Shift key, placing the tip of the mouse pointer on the tool and holding down the mouse button. Read the tool's description in the Status bar at the bottom of the screen. If you do not want to complete the tool's action, continue holding down the mouse button as you drag off the tool, and then release the button.

You can free space on a toolbar by learning the alternate tool actions. You can then delete the tools equivalent to alternate tool actions.

Delete, rearrange, or reposition tools on the toolbar

Arrange the tools on the toolbar in the order you want. You can even drag tools from one toolbar to another. When the Customize dialog box is visible, you can rearrange, reposition, move, or copy tools on toolbars.

To rearrange, reposition, or move tools:

1. Display all the toolbars you want to modify.

2. Choose the Options Toolbars command to display the Toolbars dialog box.

3. Select the Customize button from the Toolbars dialog box. The Customize dialog box displays.

4. To rearrange tools on a toolbar, use one of the following techniques:

Rearrange	Drag a tool on a toolbar to a new location and drop it.
Insert spaces	Drag a tool one-half tool width to the right, and then drop it.
Delete	Click the tool, and then press the Delete key; or simply drag the tool off the toolbar and onto the worksheet where it will disappear.
Move	Drag the tool from one toolbar to its new location on another toolbar.
Copy	Hold down the Option key, and then drag the tool from one toolbar to another location or toolbar.
Add	Drag a tool from the Customize dialog box onto the toolbar. Select from the tool categories in the Customize dialog box.

Create custom toolbars

 You can create your own toolbar and add tools to it. Your custom toolbar is available in Excel until you delete it.

To create your own toolbar:

1. Choose the Options Toolbars command.

2. In the Toolbar Name edit box, type the name of the toolbar you want to add, and then choose the Add button.

3. The Customize dialog box appears.

   As the Customize dialog box is displayed, you can drag tools from the Tools group and drop those tools onto your custom toolbar.

Display or hide the Standard toolbar quickly

To display or hide the Standard toolbar with an extended keyboard, press ⌘+7. Each press toggles the Standard toolbar on or off. Make sure that you press ⌘+7 and not ⌘+F7.

Note: Not all Macintosh computers have the extended keyboard with the function keys.

Determine whether the chart toolbar displays

Because the chart toolbar seems to appear and disappear, it can be confusing. The chart toolbar normally displays when a chart is active; when a worksheet is active, the chart toolbar disappears. This rule is broken, however, when you show or hide the chart toolbar manually.

You can also determine whether or not the chart toolbar displays by following these steps:

■ To hide the chart toolbar so that it does not appear when a chart displays, activate a chart and hide the toolbar while the chart is active.

■ To make the chart toolbar display at all times, activate a worksheet, and then display the chart toolbar.

■ To hide the chart toolbar at all times, activate a chart, and then hide the chart toolbar.

To show or hide a toolbar, choose the Options Toolbars command, select the toolbar from the Show Toolbars list, and then select the Show or Hide button as appropriate. The Show and Hide button is the same button. The button's label changes, depending on which command is appropriate for the toolbar you selected.

Read the tools in the customizing categories

Many tools are available in the different categories of the Customize dialog box. If you do not know what a tool does, click and hold the tool face. The tool's description appears at the bottom of the Customize dialog box.

Restore or delete a toolbar

To reduce the clutter of unwanted or changed toolbars, restore built-in toolbars to their original order or delete custom toolbars. To restore any built-in toolbar or delete a custom toolbar:

1. Choose the Options Toolbars command.

2. In the Toolbars dialog box, select the toolbar you want to change.

3. If it is a built-in toolbar, select the Reset button.

4. If you select a custom toolbar, the Reset button appears as Delete.

   Be careful when you delete a toolbar, because you cannot undo the deletion.

Draw your own toolface

In addition to assigning your macros to a tool on a toolbar, you can draw your own tool or modify the face on an existing tool.

To create your own toolface, you draw a new toolface in a bitmap drawing program like MacPaint or SuperPaint and then paste the face you draw over a tool on any toolbar. Although this is easy to do, a few tips can make it easier and give you better results.

The basic steps for creating a custom toolface follow:

1. Start your bitmap drawing program, such as MacPaint or SuperPaint.

2. Draw a toolface. Do not include a border around the toolface.

3. Using the Copy and Paste function of your drawing/painting package, copy the toolface to the clipboard.

4. Switch to Microsoft Excel. You may have to quit the painting program to do this.

   While in Excel, display the Customize dialog box by choosing the Options Toolbars command and selecting the Customize button.

5. With the Customize box in view, click the toolface you want to change, and then select the Edit Paste Tool Face command to copy the toolface stored on the clipboard onto the selected face in Excel.

6. Close the Customize dialog box.

You can copy or paste toolfaces only when the Customize dialog box is displayed. During this entire operation, the Customize dialog box must be displayed as you modify a tool.

Color or modify the faces on existing or custom tools

You can change the face of any tool—whether it is a tool on a predefined toolbar or a custom tool. To change a toolface, display the toolbar containing the tool with the face you want to change. Display the Customize dialog box as described earlier in this chapter. Click the tool you want to change, and then choose the Edit Copy Tool Face command. This command is available only when the Customize dialog box is displayed.

Switch to your paint program, such as MacPaint or SuperPaint. Depending on your system version, you may have to quit Excel to do this. After you are in the paint program, choose the Edit Paste command to paste the toolface. Before you click anywhere in the background, drag the toolface to the middle of the screen. This gives you space to work on all sides of the face.

The toolface is too small to edit accurately, so use your paint program's zoom command to enlarge the image on-screen. You can use the colors and the paintbrush tools to edit the individual dots in the toolface. When you finish adding color creating a new toolface, copy exactly the same size toolface as the original you pasted.

Finally, switch back to Excel. Choose Options Toolbars and select the Customize button. Now click the tool you want to receive the new face, and then choose Edit Paste Tool Face. You can only paste a new face over tools in a toolbar; you cannot replace the faces found in the various Categories of tools in the Customize dialog box (unless you move the faces to a toolbar first).

Use the blank toolface as a template for custom toolfaces

If you draw a custom toolface that is too large, Excel compresses it to fit when it is pasted on the tool. This distorts your fantastic artwork. To make it easy to get the right size tool, select Custom from the Category list in the Customize dialog box. One of the Custom toolfaces is blank. If you copy it into MacPaint or SuperPaint, you have a square of the right size for your toolface's background. Save this as a template for future toolface designs.

Save or transfer toolbars

When you quit Excel, the current toolbars and tools are stored in the Toolbars file in the Excel Startup folder. The Excel Startup folder is located in the System folder in System 6 or in the Preferences folder inside the System folder in System 7. You can save a collection of toolbars in Excel for your later use or to give to another Excel user.

To save a collection of toolbars:

1. First, set up your new toolbars in Excel as you want.

2. Then quit Excel and return to the desktop.

3. Now copy the Toolbars file and give the copy another name, such as Business Toolbars.

   You can have many toolbar files saved with different names.

When you want to use one of these toolbar collections, quit Excel and use the File Copy command to copy your *special* file to the name Toolbars in the Excel Startup folder. Restart Excel, and you'll get the new toolbars.

To transfer your collection of toolbars to another Excel user, you can copy your Toolbars file over the top of their Toolbars file and then start Excel. If the other user wants to keep his or her original toolbars, rename that person's Toolbars file to Toolbars Backup or a similar name. Then it can be renamed as Toolbars when the user wants to return to the original collection of toolbars.

4

Entering Data

After the trials of building a worksheet are finished, the mundane work of entering data begins. This chapter offers several tips on making data entry easier and faster, whether you work with numbers, dates, or text.

Enter the current date or time

Enter the current date into a cell by pressing ⌘+- (hyphen). This key combination enters the serial number for the date and formats that serial number as a date. Excel uses the date from your computer's internal clock and formats the date in standard date format.

Enter the current time in a cell by pressing Shift+⌘+; (semicolon). This enters the date-time serial number into the cell and formats the number as a time. Excel uses the time from your computer's internal clock and formats the time in standard time format.

Copy the value from the cell above

To avoid wasting time typing entries that are the same as those of the cell above in a database or column of entries, simply copy the value from the cell above by pressing Shift+⌘+" (quotation mark). If you want to copy a formula from the cell above, you can use a similar key combination; ⌘+' (apostrophe) copies a formula from the cell above and adjusts the formula to the new location (it makes the formula relative to its new location). You can extend a formula to the remaining cells in a column by using this key combination.

Enter blocks of data or formulas into multiple cells simultaneously

If you need to enter a number, date, text, or formula into more than one cell at the same time, you can do so quickly by using the following technique.

To enter data or a formula into multiple cells simultaneously, follow these steps:

1. Select all the cells in which you want to enter the number, date, text, or formula. The cells do not need to be adjacent.

2. Type the number, date, text, or formula into the formula bar.

3. Press Option+Return.

The result is the same as if you entered the data or formula into one cell and then used Edit Copy and Edit Paste to copy it into the other cells. Relative references in formulas adjust to their new locations just as if they were copied and pasted.

Caution: Make sure that you do not press ⌘+Return, a similar key combination used for array formulas.

Use group edits to enter data in multiple worksheets

Enter data in multiple worksheets at the same time by using Excel's group edit feature. With group edit on, data you enter in one sheet is simultaneously entered into other sheets in the group at the same location.

To use group edit, follow these steps:

1. Open or unhide all the worksheets in which you want to enter data and activate the specific worksheet in which you want to work.

2. Choose the Options Group Edit command.

3. In the Group Edit dialog box that appears, select the worksheets on which you want your entries duplicated.

   You can select more than one worksheet by clicking one worksheet and then using ⌘+click to select additional worksheets.

4. Choose OK. Each worksheet's name is appended with [Group] to indicate that you are in group edit mode.

5. Enter your data in the cells of the active worksheet.

   The same data is entered in the corresponding cells of other worksheets in the group as you fill in the active worksheet.

After you finish entering your data, exit the group edit mode by activating any other worksheet.

Change numbers appearing as text into numeric values

Numbers in files taken from other PC applications or downloaded from mainframe applications may appear in your file as text. This may be caused be formatting limitations in specific applications such as Lotus 1-2-3 or by an incorrectly written report generator from a mainframe.

Such numbers are preceded by an apostrophe ('), caret (^), or quotation mark ("). Some functions in Excel may not be able to coerce these text-numbers back into numerals, and math or worksheet errors result.

To change text-numbers into numeric values, type a 0 (zero) into a blank cell and then copy that cell by using Edit Copy. Now select all the cells containing text-numbers. Choose the Edit Paste Special command to display the Paste Special dialog box. Select the Paste Values option and the Operation Add option. Then choose OK.

This operation adds zero to the values in all selected cells. The values in the cells do not change, but all the selected text-numbers are forced to become numeric values so that the addition will work. (If you must perform this conversion frequently, you may want to record a macro for it.)

If your text-numbers are preceded by a quotation mark (") or a caret (^) instead of the apostrophe, you can use another technique to convert them. Select all the cells containing text-numbers, and choose the Formula Replace command. In the Find What edit box, type the character you want removed—for example, type " to remove the quotation mark.

Do not type anything in the Replace With edit box. This removes the character preceding the number. You may want to use the Find Next and Replace options to test the procedure for the first one or two occurrences. After you are satisfied it works correctly, choose the Replace All command to complete the procedure.

Force leading zeros to appear

Although it's usually a time-saver, Excel's automatic number formatting can get in the way if you enter numbers that act like text, such as a part number or a telephone number. Your company, for example, may use part numbers such as the following:

08597A
019875
005678

The problem with such numbers is that Excel strips the leading zeros from all numbers that do not contain a text character. One solution is to use a custom numeric format on any cells in which such numbers are to be entered, such as the following:

000000

This format ensures that a zero acts as a placeholder for every digit. This format also is useful for entering ZIP codes that begin with zeros, such as those in Massachusetts.

Create a series of entries quickly by using drag-and-drop

 Excel 4's drag-and-drop feature can be used to extend numeric, date, and text series (such as those shown in fig. 4.1) automatically. To create a series of text labels that indicate quarters of a year, for example, type **Q1**, **Qtr 1**, or **Quarter 1** into the first cell in the series. Then select the cell, and drag the fill-handle to the right by as many cells as you need filled with labels. As rows 14, 15, and 16 show, Excel understands that you are filling in quarters and repeats the series after the fourth quarter—starting with Q1 again.

If you need a series of sequential dates, such as the date series shown in figure 4.1, type the first date in the cell at the far left, and then drag the fill-handle to the right by as many cells as you need filled with dates. As row 18 shows, the first date (or *seed date*) you entered increases by one day per additional cell filled.

To create a date series that uses dates falling on the same day of the month (for example, the first of the month), type the first two dates as shown in the "Before" section of figure 4.1. If the calculated date from the series is greater than the last day in a month (such as when you begin with the date 1/30/93, which cannot produce a February equivalent, 2/30/93), drag-and-drop enters the last day of that month.

To enter a series containing a combination of text and numbers, you must keep the numbers at the end of the text. Enter the first text label, and follow it with the first number in the series. The text label and number can be separated by one or more spaces.

You can extend the entry Product 1, for example, into Product 2, Product 3, and so on. After entering the first combination of text and numbers, drag the fill-handle of this entry to create an on-going series. (Refer to rows 10, 11, 21, and 22 of figure 4.1.)

Finally, you can extend any numeric series, including one containing two or three entries. If you use two or three entries, Excel finds a trend and repeats it in as many cells as you drag across. If you begin with only one number, Excel simply copies the number into the remaining cells of your selection.

If you do not see the fill-handle at the lower-right corner of the selected cell, choose the Options Workspace command and select the Cell Drag-and-drop check box. Then choose OK.

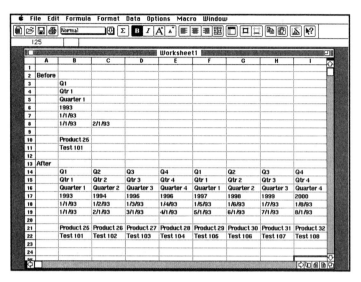

Fig. 4.1 *A series of values, dates, and text labels shown before and after using Excel's drag-and-drop series feature.*

Use drag-and-drop to enter years and quarters as titles

A series of year and quarter labels such as that shown in figure 4.2 can be useful in many business reports. Excel 4 enables you to quickly create this type of heading without retyping quarter titles or years by using Drag-and-Drop. To do so, you must first turn on Drag-and-Drop by choosing the Options Workspace command and checking the Cell Drag-and-Drop check box in the dialog box that appears.

To create your first year's titles, follow these steps:

1. Select the first cell that is to contain a quarter label, and type one of the quarter titles Excel 4 recognizes: **Q1**, **Qtr 1**, or **Quarter 1**.

2. Select this cell, and drag it to the right by three more cells. Then release the mouse button.

Excel enters the titles for quarters 2, 3, and 4 in those three cells.

3. Select the cell above the one containing the first quarter label, and type the year.

4. Select this first year cell and the three cells to the right that are above the next three quarter titles. Click the Center in Selection tool on the Standard toolbar, or choose the Format Alignment command and select the Center Across Selection option. Then choose OK.

   This procedure creates a block of cells, two rows high by four columns wide, containing the first year and the four quarter titles. The Before section in figure 4.2 shows the result of these steps.

5. Select this two-by-four block of cells, and drag the fill-handle to the right by as many sets of four cells as there are years covered in your report. Release the mouse button after you select the cells you need.

The first two-by-four block of cells is duplicated across the entire selection, but the year is increased by one every four cells. Figure 4.2 shows what this extension looks like in the After section.

Use the Glossary add-in feature to enter repetitive text, numbers, or formulas

If you frequently need to enter long titles, formulas, numbers, phrases, or descriptions, use the Edit Glossary command that comes as an add-in feature to Excel. The glossary enables you to store long text strings or numbers and enter them by typing a short abbreviation. Glossary entries also are useful to ensure that descriptions or phrases are typed correctly.

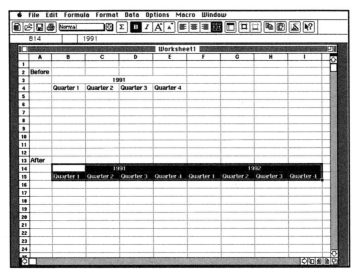

Fig. 4.2 *Year and quarter headings shown before and after using the drag-and-drop centering feature.*

To add text or data to Excel's glossary, follow these steps:

1. Type the text, formula or number into a cell or range of cells, and then select all the cells you want stored under a single abbreviation in the glossary.

2. Choose the Edit Glossary command.

3. In the Name edit box, type a short abbreviation to identify this entry.

4. Choose the Define button to add the contents of the cell or range to the glossary. After the dialog box reappears, you can define more entries or choose the Close button.

To enter an item stored in the glossary in a cell of your worksheet, follow these steps:

1. Select the cell where you want the entry to appear.

2. Choose the Edit Glossary command. The Glossary dialog box appears.

3. Select the abbreviation for the text you want from the Glossary entries list. The first portion of the glossary entry you select appears at the bottom of the dialog box.

4. Choose Insert.

To use the Glossary feature, you must install the Glossary add-in. To install the add-in, refer to the tip "Install the free add-ins that come with Excel" in Chapter 1.

Spell-check words in formulas by using the formula bar

Excel does not spell-check words in cells containing a formula. To check the spelling of a word within a formula, select the cell so that the formula appears in the formula bar. Select the word or words that you want to spell-check by highlighting them in the formula bar, and then choose the Options Spelling command.

Use tabs in your formulas

If you enter complex formulas, you may find it convenient to use tabs within those formulas. Tabs can help you break the formula into logical parts, making it easier to decipher the formula later. When entering a formula, press ⌘+Option+Return to start a new line within the formula bar. Then press ⌘+Option+Tab to indent the next line. When finished, your complex formula should appear like the following example:

```
=ROUND(
    A5/C3+(
        A200*C3
)
)
```

Programmers may find this layout more pleasing to the eye as well as easier to understand. Each section of the formula is clearly separated by the parentheses that match the parts.

Freeze formulas into values

You may want to freeze a formula so that its result does not change. This replaces the formula in the cell with the value of the formula's result. Freezing formulas can be useful if your worksheet changes based on information in other worksheets, dates, or other formulas that are updated frequently. You also may want to freeze a formula so that no further calculations are made.

To freeze a formula or a range of the worksheet containing formulas, follow these steps:

1. Select the cells containing the formula.

2. Choose the Edit Copy command.

3. Keeping the same selection, choose the Edit Paste Special command.

4. Select the Paste Values and the Operations None options.

5. Choose OK.

   The values now replace the original formulas from which they are calculated.

Another method, useful for individual cells, is to highlight the entire formula inside the formula bar and then press ⌘+= (equal sign) to calculate the formula. Press Return when finished. This converts the formula to its result and thereby freezes the formula. You can do this for an entire formula, or just a portion of it.

Format your worksheet to display the current date or time

If you need for a worksheet or report to show the current date or time, type the following function in the cell where you want the date or time to appear:

=NOW()

This function returns the date and time from your computer's clock every time the worksheet recalculates. If you want to force it to update, press the Calculate key, F9, or its shortcut, ⌘+= (equal sign).

Format the cell by using the Format Numbers command in the date or time format you need. The NOW() function recalculates to display the current date and time each time the worksheet recalculates. Press ⌘+= (equal sign) to force a recalculation. If you want to freeze this date/time so that it doesn't change, use the method described in the previous tip.

If the date and time does not display because the cell is not wide enough, use the following formula:

=TEXT(NOW(),"mmm d, yy")

This formula converts the date/time serial number returned by NOW() into text by using the format described by "mmm d, yy". You can put any predefined or custom numeric format within the quotation marks to get the date or time format you want. Because the date or time is text, it can extend beyond cell boundaries and can be formatted by using the same methods you would to format any text. The date and time continues to update whenever the worksheet is recalculated.

Check data by using custom range formats

You can use custom range formats as a simple but effective method of making sure that values typed into a worksheet fall within a specified range. If valid numbers are between 500 and 1,000, for example, the number 450 could appear in red when typed, and a text message, "Too low", also may appear. If the number is higher than 1,000, the number may appear in green along with the text message "Too high".

To create a custom numeric format that changes the appearance of a number, depending on the number and where it falls relative to a certain set range, follow these steps:

1. Select the cells you want to format.

2. Choose the Format Number command.

3. In the Code edit box, type a custom format, as described in the following paragraphs.

4. Choose OK.

Create a code by typing in the Code edit box a conditional operator within square brackets. (The conditionals are the same as those used in formulas: <, <=, =, =>, and >.) If the number in a cell satisfies the condition, then that portion of the custom format is used.

The following custom format, for example, formats numbers greater than 1,000 as blue, numbers less than 500 as red, and all numbers in between as black:

> **[Blue][>1000]0.00;[Red][<500]0.00;[Black]0.00**

In this example, all numbers use the numeric format 0.00.

In the following example, a text message is displayed along with the number and color:

[Blue][>1000]0.00 "Too high";[Red][<500]0.00 "Too low";[Black]0.00

The column containing the number must be wide enough
to display both the number and text; if it is not, the cell
displays #### instead. Only text appears when a number is
typed if you remove the number format, 0.00, from the
code and leave only the quoted text for that portion of the
format.

Check numeric ranges by using the IF function

Use the IF function to display a text warning if a numeric
entry is out of a specified range. The following formula,
for example, can be typed in cell D6 to check the entry
in cell C6:

=IF(C6<10,"Below 10",IF(C6>20,"Above 20",""))

This formula first checks to determine whether the entry
in C6 is less than 10; if it is, the message "Below 10" appears in cell D6. If the entry in C6 is greater than or equal
to 10, the second IF function works, displaying the message "Above 20" if the number in C6 is greater than 20. If
the number in C6 is from 10 to 20, the "" at the end of the
formula ensures that no text message at all is displayed. (If
you omit the "" at the end of the formula, the word FALSE
appears when the number is from 10 to 20.)

Check date ranges by using the IF and DATEVALUE functions

Check for valid date entries by using the IF, AND, and
DATEVALUE functions. In the following example, the date
is typed in cell C8 using any of the date formats that Excel
recognizes. The formula to check the dates can then be
entered in any other cell (but if you place it near the entry
cell, you can see whether the entry is valid). Type the formula as follows:

```
=IF(AND(C8>DATEVALUE("1/31 93"),
C8<DATEVALUE("3/1/93")),"","Incorrect date")
```

The formula checks to determine whether the date in C8 is both greater than 1/31/93 and less than 3/1/93. To be valid, dates must fall in the month of February 1993. Typing a February 1993 date in C8 triggers the " " part of the formula, which displays nothing. Typing an invalid date displays the text "Incorrect date".

If you want to type the upper and lower limits into cells so that the limits can be changed more easily, use the following formula instead:

```
=IF(AND(C8>M90,C8<N90),"","Incorrect date")
```

M90 is the cell that contains the lower date limit, and N90 is the cell that contains the upper date limit. The dates can be typed into the cells using any date format that Excel recognizes.

Build a formula to check workdays and holidays

If you need to make certain that a scheduled date entered into your worksheet is a workday and not a weekend or holiday, you can build a formula to check this for you.

Enter a formula such as the one that follows into a cell adjacent to the cell that contains the date you want to check:

```
=IF(AND(WEEKDAY(C8)<>7,WEEKDAY(C8)<>1,
ISERROR(MATCH(C8,Holidays,0))),"OK","Non-Workday")
```

In this example, the cell containing the date to check is C8. A list of holidays has been entered into a column on the worksheet and given the range name Holidays by using the Formula Define Name command. These dates are typed using any date format that Excel recognizes.

Three conditions are checked to determine whether a date is a workday. The WEEKDAY(C8)<>7 part of the formula checks that the date is not a Saturday. WEEKDAY(C8)<>1 checks that the date is not a Sunday. The ISERROR and MATCH combination is only true when the date is not found in the named range Holidays. The AND function ensures that all three conditions must be true at the same time for the date to be a workday.

The MATCH function checks to determine whether C8 is in the holidays list. If it is not in the list, MATCH results in an error. But the ISERROR function turns the error of not finding a matching holiday into a TRUE. So the ISERROR and MATCH combination result in TRUE when the date is not found in the list of holidays.

Check workdays and holidays by using the NETWORKDAYS function

Another, easier method of checking workdays is by using one of the analysis functions that can be added into Excel 4. Among the Analysis ToolPak add-ins is the NETWORKDAYS function. This function was designed to check the number of workdays that occur between certain dates, but it also can be used to check whether a date is a holiday. (You can open the Analysis ToolPak add-in by using either the Add-In Manager or the File Open command.)

To enter the NETWORKDAYS function, select the cell you want to contain the function, and then choose the Formula Paste Function command. In the dialog box that appears, select NETWORKDAYS from the Paste Function list, and select the Paste Arguments check box. Choose OK. The function is pasted in the selected cell as follows:

=NETWORKDAYS(Start_date,End_date,Holidays)

Edit this function into a formula, as in the following:

=IF(NETWORKDAYS(C8,C8,Holidays)=1,"Ok","Non-workday")

In this example, C8 is the cell containing the date being checked and is used for both the start and end date. Holidays is the named range containing the list of holidays. If C8 contains a valid workday, NETWORKDAYS returns 1, because it is a single workday. This causes OK to appear.

Check data entries against a list by using MATCH

If you enter part numbers, descriptions, or other items into a worksheet, you need to make sure that they are entered and spelled correctly. This is especially important if you use the Formula Find command to find the same spelling later or must find, extract, or analyze data in a database.

You can use the MATCH function to check entered data against values in a list. Unlike similar functions, the MATCH function does not return a next-closest match, but can be set to indicate when no exact match is found. The list containing valid entries to be checked against can be in any order. (It need not be in ascending order, as some functions require.)

In the following example, the data being checked is in cell B22. The formula can be entered in any other cell. If B22 contains an entry that is not found in the named range List, the text "Not in list" appears. If the contents of B22 is found in the list, "OK" is displayed instead. The formula is entered as follows:

=IF(ISERROR(MATCH(B22,List,0)),"Not in list","OK")

The MATCH formula uses the following form:

```
MATCH(lookup_value,lookup_array,match_type)
```

The `lookup_value` is the cell that contains the value being checked against the list—B22. The `lookup_array` can be a range reference to a range of cells or a named range such as the one used here, `List`. The `match_type` in this case is `0`, which tells MATCH to look only for exact matches.

Normally, if MATCH cannot find an exact match, an error results. However, you *want* to locate cases where MATCH cannot find the entry in the list, so ISERROR changes the error from MATCH into a `TRUE`. This causes `"Not in list"` to appear. If MATCH does find the entry in the list, `"OK"` appears instead. Use `""` instead of `"OK"` in the formula if you want no message displayed for valid entries.

Protect worksheets during data entry

If you have data scattered throughout a worksheet or the possibility exists of entering data in the wrong location, you may want to format the worksheet so that data can be entered only in data-entry cells.

Protecting a worksheet this way is a two-step process: First, you must select the cells to be typed in and format them as unlocked. Next, you must turn on worksheet protection. While worksheet protection is on, Excel enables you to type only in those cells that are unlocked.

To unlock cells in which you want to enter data, follow these steps:

1. Select the cells in which you want to enter data. (Use ⌘+click to select multiple cells simultaneously.)

2. Choose the Format Cell Protection command.

3. Deselect the Locked check box in the dialog box that appears. (The default setting for cells has this box selected.)

4. Choose OK.

This formats a cell so that it remains unprotected when worksheet protection is turned on. At this point, however, you can still type in any worksheet cell.

To turn on worksheet protection, follow these steps:

1. Choose the Options Protect Document command.

2. If you want to use a password so that unauthorized users cannot unlock the worksheet, type a password in the Password edit box. If you don't want to use a password, just leave the space blank and go to step 3.

3. Make sure that the Cell check box is selected.

   If you want to protect objects from moving, select the Object check box as well. If you want to keep the window from being moved on-screen, select the Window check box.

4. Choose OK.

You can now use Tab or Shift+Tab to move between unlocked cells only. Use the arrow keys or mouse to select other cells. If you attempt to type into locked cells, however, an alert box warns you that you cannot.

To remove the protection from the worksheet so that you can type in any cell, choose the Options Unprotect command. If a password was used, you are prompted for the password before you can remove the protection.

5

Formatting Text

You will probably find that you spend almost as much time formatting your worksheets as you do building them. A correctly formatted worksheet can improve the readability of your data and looks more professional, to boot. This chapter offers several timesaving tips for use in formatting your Excel worksheets.

Format multiple worksheets simultaneously

If you need to format several worksheets at the same time, save time by using the group edit feature to format them as a group.

To use group edit, follow these steps:

1. Open or unhide all the worksheets you want to format. Activate the specific worksheet in which you want to work.

2. Choose the Options Group Edit command.

3. In the Group Edit dialog box, select the worksheets you want to format. (You can select more than one worksheet by clicking the first worksheet and then using Shift+click to select additional worksheets.)

4. Choose OK.

Each worksheet's name is appended with [Group] to indicate that you are in group edit mode.

5. Format the active worksheet. Other worksheets in the group are formatted identically.

After you finish formatting the active worksheet, exit the group edit mode by activating any other worksheet.

Center multiple titles over a varying number of columns

You can use the Center Across Selection tool to center multiple titles across nonuniform selections. In figure 5.1, for example, the titles in row 4 will appear as those shown in row 16 after the former have been centered.

To center the titles across their columns, perform the following steps:

1. Type the title in the far-left cell of its section of columns.

Leave blank all remaining cells between the titles in that row.

2. Select all the cells above the columns (that is, the headings), and click the Center in Selection tool; or choose the Format Alignment command and the Center Across Selection option.

Each title moves to the right and is centered above the columns.

Add space to right-aligned columns

If you add a line (or border) down the right side of a column of right-aligned numbers, you may find that the numbers appear too close to the edge of the column. They may, in fact, almost touch the borderline.

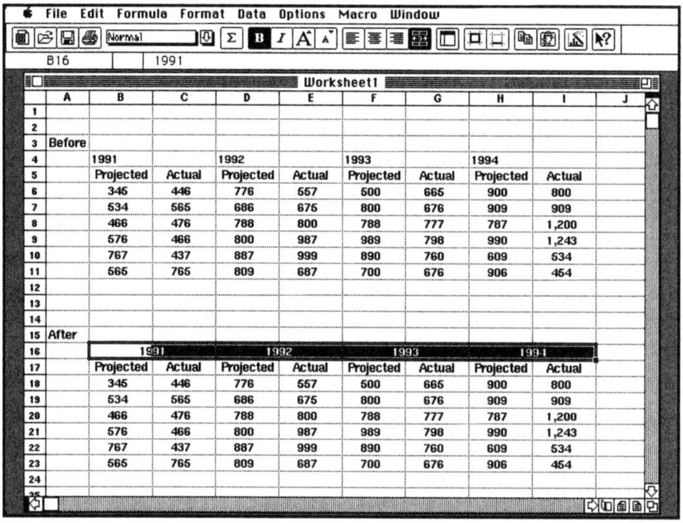

Fig. 5.1 *Headings centered across two columns by the Center in Selection tool.*

To alleviate the problem without having to center or left-align the numbers, you can use a special number format that adds extra space to the right side of the cells in the column. Choose the Format Number command, and then enter the following format into the format entry box:

#,##0.00_)_M;(#,##0.00)_M

The _M in the code adds the space of an *M* character to the end of each value in the column, providing the extra space you need between the numbers and the border. (You can add this formatting code to any of the built-in formats in the Format Numbers list.)

Save formatting time by using Styles by Example

To save time formatting cells, use *cell styles* and define them by using the *Styles by Example* method. Cell styles are names that contain all the formatting characteristics for a cell. The style named BottomLine, for example, could contain the numeric format for currency with two decimal places, set in a 12-point Helvetica bold font with a double borderline on top.

Using styles offers two advantages: First, after you have created a style, you can apply all the style's formatting characteristics to a cell by selecting the cell and choosing the style from the Style list in the Standard toolbar. Second, when you use the Format Style command to change the formatting associated with a style, all cells with that style change their formatting to match the revised style.

Creating a style by example is even easier than creating styles by using the Format Style command. To create a style by example, perform the following steps:

1. Format a cell by using the formatting of your choice for numbers, borders, fonts, patterns, alignment, and protection.

2. Select that cell.

3. Double-click in the Styles list to highlight the current style name (which may be the Normal style) and type the name you want to give to the new style.

   The new entry replaces the existing one.

4. Press Return. (The Styles list is located at the left of the Standard, Formatting, or Microsoft Excel 3 toolbar.)

The new style is now available for use when you want to apply it to a cell.

To apply a defined style, perform the following steps:

1. Select the cell or range of cells you want to format and click the down arrow to the right of the Styles list box to display the list of styles.

2. Click the style you want from the list.

3. To redefine a style, change the formatting of a cell that already has that style applied to it.

4. Reapply the same style to the newly formatted cell.

5. After you attempt to reapply that same style, Excel displays a dialog box asking whether you want to redefine the existing style.

   Affirm the action to change the existing style and all other cells using that style.

Create partial styles that don't overwrite existing formats

For some formatting chores, you may need a cell style that retains certain existing characteristics but changes other characteristics. You may, for example, want a currency style with a top double-line border to use for cells containing totals. You don't, however, want this style to change the existing font or font size of the cell. You then could use this same style on different parts of the worksheet that use different fonts.

To turn off those parts of a style that you don't want to apply, follow these steps:

1. Create the new style by using the Format Style command.

2. Choose the Format Style command.

3. Select the Style name in the Style Name box and choose the Define button.

4. Clear the check boxes in the Style Includes group for the formatting features you don't want a style to override.

5. Choose OK.

Merge styles from another worksheet

After you get used to using styles to format one worksheet, you probably will want to use the same styles on another worksheet.

To merge styles from one worksheet into another, follow these steps:

1. Open both worksheets and activate the worksheet that is to receive the styles.

2. Choose the Format Styles command and choose the Define button.

3. Choose the Merge button.

4. Select the worksheet that contains the styles you want merged.

5. Choose OK.

If the two worksheets contain styles with the same name, you're asked if you want to merge the styles anyway. If you do merge the styles, the incoming styles take precedence, overriding styles with the same name on the receiving worksheet.

Hide or display rows or columns quickly by using the extended keyboard

If you work with large reports or databases, it's often convenient to hide the rows or columns you aren't working in or don't want to print.

To hide rows, follow these steps:

1. Select a cell in each row you want hidden.

2. Use ⌘+click to select multiple cells in nonadjacent rows.

3. Press Control+9 to hide the rows.

4. You can display hidden rows by selecting cells on either side of the rows you want displayed and then pressing Shift+Control+9. (Use the 9 at the top of the keyboard, not the one on the numeric keypad.)

Note: You must have the extended Macintosh keyboard to carry out this tip. Other keyboards may not have the Control key.

To hide columns, follow these steps:

1. Select a cell in each column you want to hide.

2. Use ⌘+click to select multiple cells in nonadjacent columns.

3. Press Control+0 to hide the columns.

4. To display hidden columns, select cells on either side of the hidden columns and press Shift+Control+0. (Use the 0 at the top of the keyboard, not the one on the numeric keypad.)

Use AutoFormatting to save time

Excel 4's AutoFormatting feature can greatly speed up your work. Figure 5.2 shows examples of different formats applied by a single AutoFormat command. *AutoFormats* are predefined formats that include currency, text, borders, and color settings.

AutoFormats are especially useful for formatting lists and tables of data. Tables may include headings, row labels, and even column and row totals. Excel determines where the titles, data area, and summary rows of the data table are located and then applies a format to them.

Apply an AutoFormat by first selecting the range you want formatted. If the range is one contiguous block of data with no blank cells, you can select just one of the cells inside the table. Choose the Format AutoFormat command. Select the format you want from the Table Format list and choose OK. The dialog box shows a sample of how the format will appear.

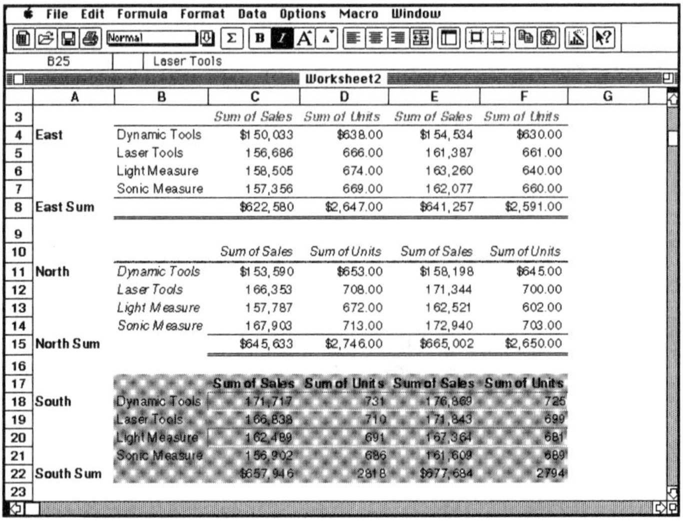

Fig. 5.2 *AutoFormats applied to a table of data.*

"Customize" your AutoFormats

AutoFormats cannot be customized, but you can modify existing AutoFormats by selecting which elements of the format are applied at any time. You can preserve existing formats in your data when you apply an AutoFormat by choosing the Options button in the AutoFormat dialog box. Deselect the check boxes in the Formats to Apply group for those formats you do not want AutoFormat to apply.

You may decide, for example, not to include the borders and fonts from the AutoFormat, retaining the data block's existing borders and fonts. This method is almost like creating a custom AutoFormat.

Apply AutoFormats with a single click

You can apply the AutoFormat you previously applied by clicking the AutoFormat tool located to the right of center on the Standard toolbar.

Change the default font by changing Normal style

 The default font used in Excel is controlled by the Normal style. To change the default font, you must redefine the Normal style.

The easiest way to change the default font is to format a cell as you want the default format to appear. Follow these steps:

1. Select the desired cell.

2. Attempt to apply a Normal style to the cell by using the Style tool or the Format Style command.

3. The cell already has a Normal style applied, but the formatting is different from the Normal definition. You are asked if you want to redefine the Normal style. Choose Yes.

Change default formats on start-up

You can create your own start-up worksheet that contains all the default formats and styles you normally use. This procedure makes the customizations available every time you create a new worksheet and start Excel.

You can avoid having to re-create the same custom formats over and over again. Creating a default start-up worksheet is described in the tip "Creating a Custom Start-Up Worksheet," located in Chapter 1, "Working with Files."

Change the colors used by AutoFormat by changing worksheet colors

The colors used by AutoFormat can be changed by changing the color palette for the worksheet. Be careful, however, because changing a color changes it wherever it's used on the worksheet. You can avoid this problem by redefining colors not used by AutoFormat as the colors you use in the worksheet.

To change a color, follow these steps:

1. Display the worksheet.

2. Choose the Options Color Palette command.

3. Click the color you want to change in the Color Palette window and select the Edit button.

4. Click the area of the Color Picker you want and choose OK.

After you return to the Color Palette dialog box, write down (or remember) the number of the color you have redefined as it appears in the list. The colors in the left column are numbered from top to bottom as 1 to 8, and the colors in the right column are numbered from 9 to 16.

If you redefine other colors on the worksheet, remember which ones they are by the order of their appearance in the custom color palette list. This procedure helps you when selecting a color from a formatting dialog box because custom colors appear with names such as Color 11. Changing the color palette also changes the colors used in 3-D Surface charts.

Use standard colors for your text, even if you redefine them in the palette

You can apply colors to your worksheet text by using the Format Font command and choosing from the colors list. You can get more than the 16 built-in colors. If you change Excel's color palette in your worksheet, you can select 16 new colors for your text. (Changing the color palette is described in the preceding tip.)

However, you still can use the 16 standard colors in your custom number formats. To apply these colors to text—even though you change the color palette—use a custom number format in the cells containing the text you want to color. Choose the Format Number command and enter the following:

    ;;;[BLUE]@

[BLUE] is any of the normal color codes, which include [BLACK], [BLUE], [CYAN], [GREEN], [YELLOW], [MAGENTA], [RED], and [WHITE]. Even if you change the color palette eliminating the color blue, using this format produces blue text.

6

CHAPTER

Formatting Dates and Numbers

Your worksheet numbers may be right, but if no one can read them and make a decision from them, you have wasted your time. To help your worksheets communicate and present polished results, format the numbers and dates the way your readers want to see them. In this chapter, you learn how to use shortcut formatting keys, how to create custom numeric and date formats, how to join text and dates for titles, and much more.

Save time with numeric format shortcut keys

Some of the most common numeric formats are built in as shortcut keys, as shown in this table:

Format	Shortcut Key
General	Shift+Control+~
#,##0.00	Shift+Control+!

continues

Format	Shortcut Key
`$#,##0.00_);($#,##0.00)`	Shift+Control+$
`0%`	Shift+Control+%
`0.00E+00`	Shift+Control+^

Notice that the keys you press with Control and Shift are the keys on the topmost row of the keyboard—right above the numeric keys.

Create custom numeric and date formats

If you don't like the numeric or date formats in the Number Format dialog box, make your own. Select the cell you want to format with a custom format and choose the Format Number command. You type the custom format you need in the Code edit box.

Any custom formats you create on a worksheet are at the end of the Format Codes list, so you only need to enter a custom format once. From then on, you can select the format from the bottom of the list.

Numeric formats, as shown in the Number Format dialog box, have four parts. The predefined formats shown in the Number Format dialog box do not show all four portions. The four portions of a custom format follow:

positive_format;negative_format;zero_format;text_format

A semicolon (;) separates the format for each part. For example, the following text formats a number with no decimal places for positive or negative values, but it does put in a comma:

`#,##0;-#,##0;0`

Zeros display as 0. Numeric formats use the characters #
to represent a digit, 0 to display a zero if there is no digit to
display, a comma (,) to mark commas, the dollar sign ($),
negative sign (–), percentage sign (%), and parentheses ( ).

Date formats do not have multiple parts. For example,
you need only *mmm d, yy,* to display a date as Oct 11, 92.
Hours, minutes, and seconds are indicated with *h, m,* and
s. The letter *m* is understood as minutes if it follows an *h.*

Look at the existing numeric and date formats in the Format Codes list to see examples of the ways the characters
can be used.

Add text to numeric formats

Add text to any numeric or date format by enclosing the
text in quotes. Type the text in the portion of the custom
format for the positive, negative, or zero value where you
want it to appear. For example:

```
#,##0 "Kph";-#,##0 "Kph";0 "Kph"
```

Add color to different signs in a numeric format

To add colors to numbers or text, include the color names
in square brackets within a portion of the custom format.
An example follows:

```
[Blue]#,##0 "Kph";[Red]-#,##0 "Kph";[Green]0 "Kph"
```

You can use the following colors:

[Black]	[White]
[Red]	[Green]
[Blue]	[Yellow]
[Magenta]	[Cyan]
[Color#]	

The # in [Color#] is the number of a color from the color palette. To display and edit the custom color palette, choose the Options Color Palette command. The colors run from 1 to 8 on the left and 9 to 16 on the right.

Format numbers so totals appear correctly

If you format numbers, their appearance changes as displayed or printed but does not change the underlying value used in calculation. For this reason, a column of formatted numbers may not add correctly—the displayed details are rounded to match the formatting, but the numbers added are the unrounded numbers stored in the cell.

To prevent this problem—and the embarrassment it can cause during presentations—choose the Options Calculation command and select the Precision as Displayed check box. When you choose OK, an alert box warns that Data will permanently lose accuracy.

This warning means that constant numbers you enter are rounded to match their formatting. In nearly all financial worksheets, you want to operate with this feature turned on.

Create a custom format to align numbers in a column

Some numeric formats cause the positive and negative numbers to fall out of alignment in a column. For example, the following text misaligns the positive and negative numbers when a column is left-aligned:

```
#,##0;<#,##0>;0
```

This misalignment occurs because the negative number has a trailing character—in this chase the left angle bracket (>). To compensate for characters that may be missing between different portions of a format, use the underscore character (_) to indicate an invisible place-holder.

The underscore character indicates to Excel to leave a blank space as wide as the character that follows the underscore. For example, to correct the preceding format you should use the following:

```
#,##0_>;<#,##0>;0
```

Create custom date formats to show abbreviations or full spellings

 Custom dates change depending on the number of letters used to indicate the day, month, or year portion. For example, see the following table:

Format	Produces
m/d/yy	8/6/93
mm/dd/yyyy	08/06/1993
mmm d, yyyy	Aug 6, 1993
mmmm d, yyyy	August 6, 1993

You can even show a day of the week with the following:

```
dddd, mmm d, yy
Friday, Aug 6, 93
```

To add text, use a format such as the following:

```
"Today is "dddd, mmmm d, yyyy
Today is Friday, August 6, 1993
```

Add dot leaders or dot trailers to numbers

 With a custom number format, you can add dot leaders or trailers to your numeric values. These characters can be useful for formatting tables. The following list describes these custom formats and shows examples of their results:

Format	Example
#.##*.	9.52....................................
*.#.##	....................................9.52

Transfer custom formats to another worksheet

If you use many custom formats, it's painful to retype all the custom formats in each new worksheet. Luckily, you don't have to.

To transfer custom formats, follow these steps:

1. In the worksheet with the custom formats, count how many custom formats you want to transfer. (Remember that those custom formats are listed at the bottom of the Format Codes list in the Number Format dialog box.)

2. In a blank area of the same worksheet, select a range with a cell for each custom format you want to transfer.

3. Type a number into each cell—the value doesn't matter for dates or numeric formats.

4. Format each cell with different custom formats you want to transfer. The order doesn't matter.

5. To transfer the formats, select the range of custom formats you have just created and choose the Edit Copy command.

6. Activate the worksheet to receive the custom formats.

7. Select a blank area of the receiving worksheet and choose the Edit Paste Special command.

8. From the Paste Special dialog box, choose the Formats option, and then choose OK.

The custom formats you pasted in now appear at the bottom of the lists in the Number Format dialog box.

Add custom number formats to your startup worksheet

Chapter 1 describes ways to create a new startup worksheet that contains your own custom settings. This worksheet can replace the default startup sheet when you use the File New command and when you first start Excel.

Try adding your custom number formats to the startup worksheet, along with the style and other settings. Refer to Chapter 1 for more details on creating and saving your new startup sheet.

Fit dates and numbers in a narrow cell

You probably have faced this situation numerous times before—you get one part of your worksheet formatted just the way you want it, but the column widths are too narrow for another part of the worksheet. The numeric and date results in these too narrow cells display as ####.

To display a number, date, or formula result in a cell that is too narrow, use the TEXT( ) function to convert the value into text. Because text can extend beyond the cell borders, a value wider than its cell can still display.

The format for the TEXT function is as follows:

TEXT(value,format_text)

The value argument can be a number, serial date number, reference to a cell, or formula that results in a number or serial date number. The format_text argument is any numeric or date format that can be used in the Number Format dialog box; it can be a predefined format or a custom format, like those described in the preceding tip.

For example, this formula displays the value in cell B6 as text in the currency format:

`=TEXT(B6,"$#,##0_);($#,##0);0_0")`

If you want a formula to directly show its result as text, put the formula as the value argument:

`=TEXT(A12*B36,"$#,##0_);($#,##0);0_0")`

A date text may appear as

`=TEXT(NOW(),"mmm d, yy")`

to show today's date or

`=TEXT(B12+5,"mmm d, yy")`

to show the date five days after the date in cell B12.

There is a detriment to using this method. If directly evaluated by one of the standard math operators, such as + − * or /, a text number will be used as a number. But if a cell containing a text number is used in the SUM function, the text number is evaluated as a zero. The tip "Change numbers appearing as text into numeric values" in Chapter 4 explains how to work around this problem.

Join text to a date or number and display it in a narrow cell

One advantage to converting numbers or dates into text is that you can join the number or date with text for use in a title. For example, if you need a phrase or title such as the following:

Report date is May 30, 1993

where May 30, 1993 is the day the worksheet is opened and printed, you can use a formula such as the following:

```
="Report date is "&TEXT(NOW(),"mmm d, yy")
```

The text in quotes is joined to the text date with the concatenation operator, &. Notice that in the example, an extra space is added after the word *is*. This space creates the space in the resulting concatenated string.

Use pictures to display formulas or dates as titles

The preceding tip shows how to overcome the column width limitation for a column of values by converting the values to text. Another way to accomplish this task, which is especially useful for headings and titles, is to enter the title in a remote area of the worksheet and format it as desired. You can expand the column width of its cell if necessary. Now use the Camera tool located on the Utility toolbar to take a picture of this cell. Move the picture into place as the column heading or title.

Hide zeros throughout the worksheet

To hide zeros throughout a worksheet, choose the Options Display command. Clear the Zero Values check box. Numbers do not appear in the worksheet or in a print but can be seen in the formula bar when a cell containing a zero is

selected. The value of zero still exists in the cell so it can be
used for math.

Hide zeros in specific cells by formatting

To hide zeros in selective portions of a worksheet, format
that portion with a custom numeric format that hides
zeros. To hide a zero, put in the semicolon that precedes
the zero format but do not put in a format. For example:

```
#,##0;-#,##0;
```

Enter this custom format by selecting a cell or range and
choosing the Format Number command to display the
Number Format dialog box. In the Code edit box, type the
custom format and choose OK.

Hide numbers selectively

As the preceding tip illustrates, a custom numeric format
uses semicolons to separate the four different types of
formats. To hide a value of a specific sign, format cells
with a custom format that has the appropriate semicolons
but does not have a format for that sign.

For example, the following custom format hides negative
numbers because there is a positive format before the first
semicolon and a negative format after the second semicolon. But in the negative portion, between the first and
second semicolon, there is no format:

```
#,##0;;0
```

To hide a number completely but keep it available for
formulas, you can change the character font to the same
color as the screen background or use the following
custom format:

```
;;;
```

Selecting a cell with the contents hidden by color or formatting still enables you or another operator to see the cell contents in the formula bar.

Protect cells from change

One common way to introduce mistakes into a valid worksheet is to accidentally type in the wrong cell. This action may overwrite a constant or a formula; if left, it can cause incorrect results. To prevent yourself or others from typing in the wrong cells, lock all cells except those in which you want to enter data.

Protecting a worksheet is a two-step process. You format the cells you want to unlock and then you protect the worksheet.

Follow these steps:

1. Format the cells you want as changeable cells by selecting the cell, choosing the Format Cell Protection command, and clearing the Locked check box.

2. Choose OK.

   A cell's locked or unlocked formatting does not take effect until worksheet protection is turned on.

3. After you format the changeable cells as unlocked, choose the Options Protect Document command.

4. In the Protect Document dialog box that appears, type a password in the Password edit box to prevent unauthorized users from unprotecting the worksheet.

5. Select the Cells, Objects, or Windows check boxes, depending on what you want locked.

   If you lock windows, they are not moveable on-screen.

6. Choose OK.

   To make sure that you didn't mistype, you will be
   asked to retype the same password. Don't forget your
   password.

Note: Upper- and lowercase letters make a difference in
the password, so remember how you typed it.

Unprotect a document by choosing the Options
Unprotect Document. When asked for a password, type
one if one was used. If you did not use a password, just
choose OK.

Format numbers to display thousands or millions

You can round a number up by a thousand or a million for
display and printing, but still have the real number in the
cell for calculations if you use the correct custom format.
For example, with the number 999,888,777 you can get the
results in the following table:

Format	Display or Print	Magnitude
###,	999889	Thousands
###,,	1000	Millions

7

Editing and Building Formulas

Formulas are the heart and soul of your worksheet. If you build lots of worksheets or macros in Excel, you will appreciate any tricks that can help you work faster and with fewer errors. This chapter describes tips that help you duplicate, enter, and edit formulas.

Change cell references between relative and absolute quickly

You don't have to type in the dollar signs to change a cell reference between relative and absolute reference. Any time the insertion point is beside a cell reference, whether you are entering or editing, you can press ⌘+I to enter cell references. Each press of the key cycles it to another combination of dollar signs.

There are four combinations, as you can see in the following example:

A1
$A$1
$A1
A$1

Create exact copies of formulas

At times you will need to experiment with a formula by changing or editing it, but you want to be safe and leave the original formula untouched. Copying and pasting commands to move a formula to another cell and experimenting on the formula there won't work because copying and pasting the formula adjusts the relative cell references.

To create an exact copy of a formula in a new cell, without the formula adjusting, you can use two methods. If there is a blank cell under the cell that contains the formula, create an exact copy by selecting the cell under the formula and pressing ⌘+' (apostrophe). This copies the formula without adjusting cell references.

Caution: Be careful to not use this shortcut key when you enter data. In most data entry situations, such as entering data in a database, you will want the relative references of a formula to adjust—which this shortcut does not accomplish.

Another way to copy a formula exactly is to select the cell that contains the formula. Then click in front of the equal sign in the formula bar and drag to the end of the formula so that the entire formula is selected. Now choose the Edit Copy command. Next, select the cell where you want the formula to be copied and choose the Edit Paste command. This pastes the formula without adjusting relative cell references.

Copy and paste within the formula bar

You can cut, copy, and paste in a formula bar, just as you would in a miniature word processor. This can be very helpful when you build complex formulas that share a common part or when you reorganize pieces in a formula. To cut or copy, select the portion in the formula bar that you want to cut or copy, and then choose the Edit Cut command (⌘+X) or the Edit Copy command (⌘+C).

To paste in the same formula, just move the insertion point to where you want to paste and choose the Edit Paste command (⌘+V). To paste into another formula, select the cell that contains that formula, move to where you want to paste the insertion point in its formula bar, and choose the Edit Paste command (⌘+V).

Copy and paste within Excel dialog boxes

Sometimes you can save time if you copy and paste in dialog boxes. Although the Edit commands don't work in dialog boxes, the editing shortcut keys do.

If you need to find all occurrences of a complex range name or a portion of a formula, for example:

1. Use the previous tip to copy a portion of a formula or text into the Clipboard.

2. Display the dialog box into which you want to paste the formula or text.

3. Select the edit box into which you want to paste and press ⌘+V.

4. To copy from within a dialog box, select the characters and press ⌘+C.

5. To cut from within a dialog box, select the characters and press ⌘+X.

Paste in function arguments rather than memorizing them

When you use one of Excel's multitude of worksheet functions, it's hard to remember the order in which arguments are placed in parentheses. Thank heavens you don't have to!

Instead, choose the Formula Paste Function command (Shift+F3) to paste the function and its arguments in. Select the function you want from the Paste Function list. Before you choose the OK button, make sure that the Paste Arguments check box is turned on. It makes Excel paste in the function, and it inserts a text description of what goes in each argument in the parentheses.

Change multiple formulas with the Replace command

When you work with similar formulas in worksheets or macros, speed up your work by using the Formula Replace command instead of retyping each formula. For example, in a macro you may have many SET.VALUE functions that set the defaults for a dialog box. The FORMULA functions that transfer data out of the same dialog box use almost the same form and may act on the same references or range names.

Rather than entering all the SET.VALUE functions and then retyping all the FORMULA functions, copy the SET.VALUE functions to where you want the FORMULA functions. Select all the SET.VALUE functions, and then use the Formula Replace command to replace SET.VALUE with FORMULA. Make sure that you have the Look at Part option selected before you choose OK.

Recalculate a portion of a worksheet

You can recalculate a portion of a worksheet by following these steps:

1. Make sure that the worksheet is in manual calculation mode before you start. This is found under the Options Calculation command.

2. Select the area that you want to affect; then choose the Formula Replace command.

3. In the Find What edit box, type an equal sign (=).

4. To recalculate the area without recalculating the rest of the worksheet, type an equal sign (=) in the Replace With edit box.

5. Make sure that the Look at Part option is selected; then choose OK.

The selected area recalculates because the Replace command actually re-enters each formula when it replaces the equal sign.

Paste names from other worksheets into formulas

Names are a valuable ally when you create manageable worksheets—and they're indispensable when you write macros. After you have named cells or ranges on your worksheet, it is very easy to select them by pressing the Goto key, F5, or typing ⌘+G.

To easily paste a name into a formula, choose Formula Paste Name, select the name, and choose OK.

To use information from one worksheet in another, you find you want to paste a name from one worksheet into another. The way to do that isn't obvious.

To paste a name from one worksheet into another, follow these steps:

1. Select the cell and type an equal sign—or if you are in the middle of a formula, move the insertion point to where you want the name inserted.

2. Activate the worksheet or macro sheet that contains the names by choosing the sheet from the Window menu. (The Window menu works even though you are in the middle of editing.)

3. Press the F3 key, or choose the Formula Paste Name command.

4. When the Paste Name dialog box appears, select the name you want to paste and choose OK.

5. Continue to build the formula or switch between worksheets.

6. When you press Return, the worksheet or macro sheet with the formula reactivates and shows the finished formula.

The Paste Name dialog box will not display if no names are defined on the active worksheet.

Change names with the Changer add-in

Unless you are perfect or very well-practiced, you probably will change your mind about the abbreviations you used for some names in large worksheets. To manually change names, you need to redefine the new names, change all the formulas that used the name, and then delete the old name. And then hope that you corrected all the instances!

Rather than going through all that work, use the Changer add-in that comes with Excel. To change names with the Changer:

1. Choose the Formula Change Name command.

2. When the Rename a Name dialog box appears, select the name you want changed from the From list.

3. In the To box, type the new name, and then choose Rename.

The Changer redefines the name, replaces all instances in formulas that used that name, and then deletes the old name.

One condition exists: if you created the names from text labels in cells using the Formula Create Names command, the text labels do not update to reflect the new names.

If you do not see the Change Name command on your Formula menu, you need to use the Add-in Manager to add Changer. Changer is one of many free add-in programs that come with Excel and add features. Refer to the tip "Install the free add-ins that come with Excel" in Chapter 1 for information on installing add-in programs.

If your computer does not have the Macro Library folder or the Name Changer file, get your original Excel installation disks and reinstall Excel using the Custom installation option. You do not need to reinstall all of Excel, only the library.

Calculate part of a formula to check for errors

When a large formula in a worksheet or macro sheet produces an error, sometimes it is difficult to find which part of the formula is causing the problem. To make it easier to see which part of the formula calculates incorrectly, calculate parts of the formula right in the formula bar. Any piece of a formula or function that can be calculated by itself can be calculated. In other words, it must be a piece that could stand alone and be calculated.

To calculate part of a formula:

1. Select the cell that contains the formula.

2. Click in the formula bar or press ⌘+U (or F2), and select the piece of the formula you want to calculate.

Figure 7.1 shows a portion of a formula selected.

3. Press ⌘+= or the F9 key to see the result of the selection.

   Figure 7.2 shows the same portion after pressing ⌘+=.

4. When you finish examining the partial results, press the Escape key so that the altered formula does not replace the original formula.

	A	B	C	D	E	F	G
1							
2			1/1/92		2/1/92		
3			Sum of Sales	Sum of Units	Sum of Sales	Sum of Units	
4	East	Dynamic Tools	$150,033	$638.00	$154,534	$630.00	
5		Laser Tools	156,686	666.00	161,387	661.00	
6		Light Measure	158,505	674.00	163,260	640.00	
7		Sonic Measure	157,356	669.00	162,077	660.00	
8	East Sum		$622,580	$2,647.00	$641,257	$2,591.00	
9							
10			Sum of Sales	Sum of Units	Sum of Sales	Sum of Units	
11	North	Dynamic Tools	$153,590	$653.00	$158,198	$645.00	
12		Laser Tools	166,353	708.00	171,344	700.00	
13		Light Measure	157,787	672.00	162,521	602.00	
14		Sonic Measure	167,903	713.00	172,940	703.00	
15	North Sum		$645,633	$2,746.00	$665,002	$2,650.00	
16							
17							
18	TOTALS		$1,268,213	$5,393	$1,306,259	$5,241	
19							
20							
21							

Fig. 7.1 *Select the portion of a formula you want to calculate.*

When you troubleshoot, it is usually best to begin calculating smaller inside portions of a formula and work outward to the entire formula. After you find a piece that produces an error, (shown by a #error message) you can examine that individual piece more closely.

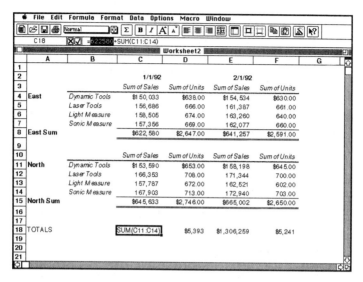

Fig. 7.2 *Pressing ⌘+= calculates only the selected part of the formula.*

Note: This will not work correctly in a few situations—for example, when the selected piece refers to an unopened worksheet or when a selected macro function requires the worksheet to be active when the selected function calculates.

Select cells leading into or out of a formula

When troubleshooting formulas, it's often helpful to know which formulas or data feed into the selected formula (precedence) and which formulas depend on the selected formula (dependence). This knowledge can help you track down where an error came from or went.

One way to see the precedence or dependence cells is to select the formula in question and choose the Formula

Select Special command. Select the Precedents or Dependents options. For each, you can choose to see only those that directly precede or depend, the Direct Only option, or all cells that precede or depend, which is the All Levels option.

To see what feeds in or out of a formula, select the formula and then press one of the shortcut keys in the following table:

To See	Press
Cells feeding directly into formula	⌘+[
All cells that eventually feed in	⌘+Shift+{
Cells that depend directly on formula	⌘+]
All cells that eventually depend	⌘+Shift+}

A final way to select precedents (cells that feed directly into a formula) is to double-click on the cell that contains the formula. This automatically highlights the cell that feeds directly into that formula. You can even do this with linked references.

View or print the formulas in a worksheet

In worksheets, view or print formulas by choosing the Options Display command, selecting the Formulas check box, and choosing OK. Formulas display instead of results. The column width automatically doubles to show more of the formulas. If you change a column width, you change it in the normal display also.

Press the ⌘+` key to quickly switch between the display of formulas and results. The back apostrophe (`) is located on the same key as the tilde (~).

Find the chain of connected formulas in a circular reference

Among the most difficult worksheet problems to trouble-shoot are circular reference errors. Luckily, Excel comes with an Audit add-in and the Formula Select Special commands that find the formulas involved in a circular reference.

Circular references are two or more formulas that refer back on themselves. Imagine it as a snake eating its own tail. For example, if a worksheet has the formulas A, B, and C involved in a circular reference, A uses B's results, B uses C's results, and C uses A's results.

Because all the results depend on each other, strange things can happen as the worksheet recalculates. In some cases, results keep getting larger; in other cases, results keep getting smaller, and in a few instances, nothing bad happens. In any circumstance, investigate circular reference errors to determine whether those references are benign or malignant.

When you enter a formula that closes the chain and initially creates a circular reference, an alert box appears with the message `Cannot resolve circular reference`. When you choose OK, the Status bar at the bottom of the screen shows the message `Circular: A12`, where A12 is the cell of the last entry that created the circular reference.

Do not just delete the cell shown in the Circular message. Actually, many cells may reference each other. To find all the cells in the circular error, select the cell in the Status bar and choose the Formula Select Special command. Select either the Precedents or Dependents options and the All Levels option. When you choose OK, all the cells that reference each other are selected.

To examine each formula and keep all formulas selected, press the Tab key to move between them. Look for a cell reference that refers back to itself. If, after choosing the Formula Select Special command, only the original cell is selected, its formula refers to the very cell in which it resides—it is trying to calculate a new result based on its own result.

If you have a very complicated circular reference, use the Audit add-in to get a printed report of all cells involved in the circular reference, their formulas, and their results. The Formula Worksheet Auditor command becomes available only as an add-in. Choose the Formula Worksheet Auditor command if it is available. In the Worksheet Auditor dialog box, select the Generate Audit Report option, and choose OK. In the Audit Report dialog box that appears, select only the Circular Reference check box, and then choose OK.

In very large worksheets with very bad circular errors, the circular reference error report may take as long as half an hour to generate, but it solves what can be an insidious error, and you can do something else in the meantime.

If the Formula Worksheet Auditor command is unavailable, use the Options Add-ins command to add the Worksheet Auditor add-in to Excel. The Worksheet Auditor add-in is found in the Macro Library folder. Refer to the tip "Install the free add-ins that come with Excel" in Chapter 1 for information on installing add-in programs.

Find all formulas linked to other worksheets

To find any formula linked to another worksheet, search for the exclamation mark. The exclamation mark is always used as a separator between file names and cell reference in external references.

To search, use the Formula Find command. Type ! in the Find What dialog box. Make sure that you have Look in Formulas and Look at Part options selected. Choose OK to find the next linked formula. To continue with the same search, press F7 or enter ⌘+H.

Total multiple columns or rows with AutoSum

The AutoSum tool is a very useful way of quickly summing a column or row. But it can be even faster. Enter the SUM function into multiple cells at one time. This works when you total a column if each column has the same number of cells. The columns of numbers do not have to be aligned. Just highlight all the total cells below the columns, and then *double-click* the AutoSum tool.

If you are totaling rows, all the rows must have the same number of cells. The rows do not have to be aligned. To enter multiple totals at one time, select all the cells in which you want the total, and then double-click the AutoSum tool.

8

Calculating with Formulas

In a worksheet, the formulas you work with usually duplicate the formulas or procedures you use if you work manually. But in some situations, formulas don't work as you expect, or the required formula isn't obvious. Some of the less well known formulas discussed here should help you work faster and smarter.

Don't let cell widths hamper your formulas

Some reports require very specific formatting, but this may present a problem because a large result may not fit in a narrow cell. When a number or date is too wide to fit in a cell, the cell shows ###.

To resolve this problem, put the formula in a TEXT( ) function. Figure 8.1 shows how formula results can fit in narrow cells and be aligned like text. The numbers are entered in column B. Column D contains the TEXT function that converts the B column into a text-number. Column F shows the formula that produced the text in column B. The B column cell references in the TEXT( ) functions can be complete formulas rather than a reference to a cell that contains a formula.

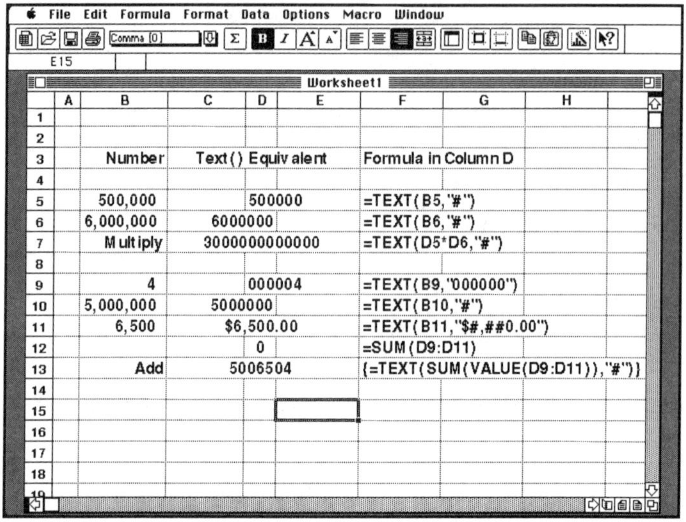

Fig. 8.1 *Use TEXT and VALUE to put numeric formulas in narrow cells.*

The TEXT( ) function converts the formula result into text that can expand beyond the edges of a narrow cell. The format for TEXT( ) is the following:

    TEXT(reference,text_format)

The preceding reference can be a formula or cell reference, and text_format is a custom format enclosed in quotes.

Chapter 6, "Formatting Dates and Numbers," describes custom formats at the beginning.

The problem that may arise is that these "numbers as text" may not be evaluated as numbers by some other formulas. The next two tips show you how to force text numbers to work in functions such as SUM( ).

Convert text-numbers into values in math operations

Excel has the unique capability of forcing (the technical term is *coercing*) text, numbers, and references into whatever form is needed by a math operation or by most functions.

In figure 8.1, for example, cells D5 and D6 appear to be numbers, but they are text. Still, they can be multiplied with a formula such as the following:

    =D5*D6

When Excel acts on each text-number individually, it has a chance to coerce each text-number into a number that can be added, subtracted, multiplied, or divided. In figure 8.1, the product of the two cells in cell D7 is converted back into text by the TEXT function so that it appears in the narrow column.

If you use a function such as SUM( ) to act on a range of cells, and some of the cells contain text-numbers, Excel doesn't have a chance to coerce the individual cells into numbers. Those numbers then get treated as text and are totalled as zeros. The following tip shows you how to work around this problem.

Calculate functions that work on text-numbers

Text-numbers solve the problem of fitting large numbers or formula results into narrow cells, but occasionally they cause a problem downstream because another formula or function can't use them as a number. Following is a way to to solve that problem.

Text-numbers are evaluated one at a time—for example, if the following formula were used in figure 8.1, Excel would coerce each text-number into a real number and perform the math operation:

=D9*D10

A problem arises when a range is evaluated by a function, as shown in cell D12 (refer to fig. 8.1). The SUM in D12 totals the range in D9:D11. Notice that the total is 0. The text-values in the range were not coerced or individually evaluated and thus totalled 0. Excel's lack of coercion occurs with functions besides SUM.

To resolve this problem, force Excel to examine the contents of each cell individually by using an array formula. *Don't skip the rest of this tip! It is actually easy to do.* An array formula is a single formula that evaluates multiple cells in a range.

You need a formula that evaluates every cell in the range so each cell is coerced, and then totals all the cells. The formula to do this is in D13; note that it gives a correct total. The formula that does the total is the following:

{=TEXT(SUM(VALUE(D9:D11)),"#")}

The braces around the formula indicate that it is an *array formula.* When you type the formula into cell D13, *do not press Enter;* instead press ⌘+Enter. Array formulas display in the formula bar enclosed in braces {}. Do not type the braces. Array formulas force Excel to examine each cell in the range one at a time, and then perform the larger calculation.

The VALUE function goes through each cell in the array D9:D11. Because this is an array formula, VALUE works on each cell individually. VALUE converts each text-number into a real number. The result of VALUE is an array of three numbers. These three numbers can then be totalled by the SUM function.

Use the ROUND function to round numbers

Chapter 6, "Formatting Dates and Numbers," describes how you can make the precision (decimal places) of numbers in a worksheet match their formatted appearance with the use of the Precision as Displayed check box under Options Calculation. But sometimes you need to round just a few numbers and leave other numbers unrounded, displaying their full precision.

To round numbers, use the ROUND(number,num_digits), where number can be a number, cell reference, or formula, and num_digits is the number of decimal places you want. For example, the following formula rounds the result of B6*B9 to two decimal places:

=ROUND(B6*B9,2)

Round numbers to any number

If you need to round off to the even half dollar (or if you work for the federal government and need to round off to hundreds of millions), this tip will be helpful. In some financial and engineering calculations, you need to round numbers to partial decimals.

You may need to round $65.46 to $65.50, for example. To round a number or formula to a partial decimal, use a formula like the following:

=ROUND(65.46/0.5,0)*0.5

In this example, 65.46 needs to be rounded to the .5 level. To do this, divide 65.46 by .5, round the result to the 0 precision, and multiply the result times the .5 level. When you actually use this method, you replace the number 65.46 with a formula or a cell reference.

Round numbers up to tens, thousands, or millions

Sometimes you need to round a number up instead of down. For example, you want to round 789,534.89 to the closest thousand. To round to the left of the decimal, use a negative num_digit in the argument. For example,

=ROUND(789534.89,–3)

rounds the number to 790,000. When you actually use this formula, you replace the number 789534.89 with a formula or a cell reference.

Calculate the products or averages of two ranges in a single cell

 You can perform many math calculations in a single cell if you understand how to use array formulas. For example, in figure 8.2, the more typical method of calculating total dollars sold appears in cell E10. But this method requires first multiplying the quantity and price to produce subtotals in cells E6:E9, which takes up room on the worksheet.

If you use an array formula, you can perform many calculations on multiple ranges in one cell. The formula in E11 does the same multiplication and total as E10, but all the calculations are done in one cell. The formula in E11 appears in G11.

The formula in E11 was entered as an array formula by typing the formula in E11 without the braces {}, and entering it by pressing ⌘+Enter. (Pressing ⌘+Enter automatically enters the braces {}. They cannot be typed to create an array formula.)

The array formula works by first multiplying each cell in the C6:C9 range times the corresponding cell in the D6:D9 range. This action produces an array of the multiplication results. You can actually see these results if, after entering the formula with ⌘+Enter, you select the terms C6:C9*D6:D9 in the formula bar and press ⌘+=. The results appear in the formula bar:

=SUM({150;240;350;480})

Press Esc to preserve the original formula. Finally, the SUM function in cell E11 totals the array of multiplication results, {150;240;350;480}.

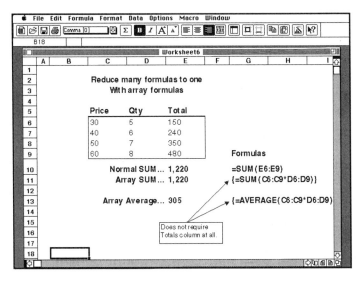

Fig. 8.2 *Use array formulas to perform calculations on ranges in a single cell.*

Cell E13 shows an average of products created with an array formula. Again, the formula must be entered with ⌘+Enter. This formula first multiplies the two ranges cell by cell. The AVERAGE function then averages the results of the multiplication.

Examples of array math used to analyze tables and data-bases appear in Chapter 12, "Sorting and Databases."

Calculate the end of the month

Excel 4 calculates the end of a month for you. You can use the DATE function so that it backs up one day from the first of the following month. Excel 4 even calculates February 29 in leap years.

The usual form of the DATE function is the following, where year, month, and day are numbers:

DATE(year,month,day)

This form results in a serial-date number that is the number of days from the beginning of the century. For example, the serial-date for Oct 11, 94 is 34,618. If the date appears as a number in the cell, use the Format Number command to change the format to a date.

To calculate the end of a month, use the following formula:

DATE(year,month+1,0)

For example, if B6 is month and C6 is the year, use this formula:

=DATE(C6,B6+1,0)

Calculate the last work day of the month

For invoice due dates, payrolls, or tax calculations, you may face the problem of trying to figure out how to calculate the last work day of each month. Use the WORKDAY function to find the last workday in a month. The WORK-DAY function finds a work day that is some specified number of work days in the future or past. The form for WORKDAY is the following:

=WORKDAY(start_date,days,holidays)

In this form, start_date is the base date from which you want to calculate a work day. The days argument is the number of work days in the future or past. (Future days are positive; past days are negative.) The holidays argument is a range on the worksheet that contains the dates of holidays, so you can create your own list of national, religious, corporate, or personal sanity holidays.

To calculate the last work day of the month, give WORK-DAY the last day of the month as the start_date, and then ask for the closest prior work day. To do this use a formula, like the following:

=WORKDAY(start_date+1,–1,holidays)

This formula works by adding one to the start_date. The –1 as the day argument asks WORKDAY to find the next prior work day. If you use the last day of the month as the start_date argument, this formula results in the last work day of the month. Combine the preceding formula with the tip that calculated the last day of a month to produce a formula that calculates the last work day of the month.

=WORKDAY(DATE(year,month+1,0)+1,–1,holidays)

The year and month arguments are integers. The holidays argument is a range that contains the dates excluded from work days.

9

Outlining, Consolidating, and Tabulating Data

When you have a lot of data, whether in a database or a worksheet format, consider using the outlining and crosstab features of Excel for compiling, analyzing, and reporting the results. Another useful feature is the Scenario Manager, which can help you manage multiple sets of input data. When you need to accumulate data from multiple worksheets, use Excel's Data Consolidate command.

Use Scenario Manager to check the results of many inputs

If you have worksheets where you need to generate different scenarios, such as the best case, worst case, and most probable case, you should investigate the

Scenario Manager. The Scenario Manager keeps named sets of input data and the output results. To rerun a scenario, all you need to do is open the Scenario Manager and select a scenario by name. You have the choice of seeing the changes in the worksheet or getting a printout of only the results and inputs.

Name your data input and result cells for a more understandable scenario summary

If you choose the Summary button in the Scenario Manager, Excel generates a summary report for you. The report shows, in the chosen scenario form, the cells in which data was changed; it also shows the results that correspond to the input changes.

If you do not use named ranges on your worksheet, the summary report from the Scenario Manager is almost inscrutable. Input cells and result cells show up in the report with their cell references, such as $B$12 or $AC$15:$AF$15. You have to have an incredible memory to use such a report, or always keep the original worksheet in front of you.

A better way of working is to name your input cells and your result cells before you generate the summary report. You can name cells manually by using the Formula Define Name command; alternatively, you can use the Formula Create Names command to create multiple names using the text labels that are in the worksheet. The summary report then includes the range names, even if you create the names after the scenarios are built and stored in the Scenario Manager.

Build an outline toolbar for easier outlines

The Standard toolbar in Excel 4 does not have the collection of tools needed for working with outlines. Display the Microsoft Excel 3 toolbar, or create a custom toolbar that contains the outline tools from the Utility category of the Customize toolbar dialog box. Perform these actions with the Options Toolbars command, and then choose the Customize option.

Print or graph an outline level

An outlined area of the worksheet can be confusing if you attempt to print or chart a selection when you have only a few of the outline levels displayed. Consider that you may have only the top two levels of row headings displayed, for example, but the outline has five levels of row headings. If you select this data and print or chart it, data from the full five levels of row headings will be used.

If you want to restrict your outline selection so charting or printing uses only the levels you have displayed, you must use the Select as Displayed tool. The Select as Displayed tool is on the Excel 3 toolbar to the left of the AutoSum tool.

The Select as Displayed tool looks like four dark cells with space in between them. To add this tool to an Excel 4 toolbar, display the Customize toolbar dialog box and drag the Select as Displayed tool from the Utility category onto a toolbar.

To print or chart only the outline level you want, display the outline with that level, select the data you want, and then click the Select as Displayed tool. (Notice that the selection changes as though the interior of cells are selected but not the space between cells.) Continue with your normal charting or printing procedure.

Use styles with outlining to format the data

A handy addition to the outlining feature is the capability to attach styles to the various levels of your outlined worksheet. Choose the Apply Styles option in the Outline dialog box to tell Excel to apply style names automatically to the various levels of the outlined worksheet. All data on the same "level" will have the same style attached; the styles will appear in the Styles list on the toolbar.

Of course, you can modify the styles after you apply them—and Excel updates all data using the modified style. Also, you can use the AutoFormat command to format your worksheet *before* outlining. The outlining styles then use the formats from the AutoFormat command—breaking down the AutoFormat formats into individual styles in the Styles list.

Create database reports with the Crosstab ReportWizard

 The Crosstab ReportWizard is one of the most exciting features to be added to Excel 4. If you work with databases or information downloaded from a mainframe, you should investigate the types of reports the Crosstab ReportWizard can build for you.

You can link reports from the Crosstab ReportWizard back to the original data so that changes in the data are reflected in the cross-tabulation. You also can drill-down on cross-tabulations to see the detail that comprises a summary.

Make sure that the Crosstab ReportWizard is installed by looking for the Crosstab command in the Data menu. You can install this add-in (located in the Macro Library folder) through the Add-In Manager. For more information, see the tip "Use Drill-Down to see the detail of a crosstab" later in this chapter.

If the Crosstab Wizard is not installed, rerun the Excel installation diskettes. Choose the Custom installation process and install only the Crosstab Wizard.

Limit the data analyzed by the Crosstab ReportWizard

The Crosstab Wizard works on the data that has the range name *Database*. If you operate the Crosstab Wizard without restrictions, it analyzes all data in the database. You may have thousands of rows of data in the database, for example, all of which the Crosstab Wizard analyzes and reports on. Besides taking additional time, this process may not produce the report you want.

To restrict the data that the Crosstab Wizard uses for analyzing and reporting, create a criteria range on the database worksheet as you do for a normal Excel database. Define the range with the Data Set Criteria command.

Enter criteria in the criteria range that describe the data you want analyzed. Before starting the Crosstab Wizard to build your report, use the Data Find command to make sure that your criteria correctly describe the data you want.

Group crosstab results into date groups such as months and quarters

If the data you are creating reports and analysis from covers a range of time, you may want to see the data analyzed according to time frames, such as days, weeks, months, quarters, and so on. You may enter sales data infrequently, for instance, but need to see it totalled into groups of weeks, months, or quarters. The Crosstab Wizard can do that for you.

After you select your Row or Column Categories that include dates, choose the Options button in the lower right corner of the Wizard. In the Category Options window that appears, the first box should show Create Column/ Row from followed by the name of the row or column that contains dates. If this database column contains dates, the next edit box is the In Groups of pull-down list. Pull down this list, which lists the different time frames by which you can group data, and choose the time group you need.

Limit time spans in crosstab reports

If you do not use a criteria range to limit the data on which the Crosstab Wizard works, you can specify a start and stop time for the data. After you select your row or column headings from the Row or Column Categories window, choose the Options button. In the Categories Option window, enter the start date in the Starting at edit box and enter the end date in the Ending at edit box.

Rebuild crosstabs quickly

With Crosstab Wizard, you can easily modify a crosstab report that you have already created in order to rebuild it with different data fields, group dates differently, or add restrictions. Make sure that the original database worksheet is open and then activate the worksheet containing the crosstab report. Choose the Data Crosstab command. When the Crosstab Wizard appears, choose the Modify Current Crosstab button.

Recalculate a crosstab rather than rebuild the report

If data in the crosstab report has changed, you don't need to completely rebuild the report. Open the worksheet containing the database and then activate the worksheet containing the crosstab report and choose the Data Crosstab command. When the Crosstab Wizard appears, choose the Recalculate Current Crosstab button.

Retrieve or use crosstab results by typing names

If you want to retrieve data from the crosstab report just by typing names, choose the Set Table Creation Options button in the final Crosstab Wizard window. The Create Options dialog box appears. Select Yes for the Define names for use in formulas? option.

When the Crosstab Wizard creates the cross-tabulation report, the entire report area has rows, columns, and the range with understandable names—that assumes, of course, that you understood the labels in your database. You can jump to one of the named ranges by pressing ⌘+G, selecting a name, and choosing OK. For example, the entire cross-tabulation report is always named Crosstab_range.

Row labels match the headings used in each row. Column labels, likewise, match column headings. You can use these names in formulas to reference specific data or use them with the ⌘+G to go to specific cells.

For example, if an entire row in the report is named Laser_Tools and an entire column is named Jun93, you can reference the data where the row and column cross by using the intersect operator—a space. If you want a cell to show two times the Laser_Tools sum for the month of June 1993, use the formula

=(Laser_Tools Jun93)*2

Notice the space in between the names Laser_Tools and Jun93.

If you want to go to the intersection of Aug93 and Grand_total, for example, press ⌘+G. Then type **Grand_total Aug93** in the Reference edit box and choose OK. Again, you must have a space between the two names to indicate that you want the cell where these two names intersect.

Use Drill-Down to see the detail of a crosstab

Many corporate developers and Microsoft Consulting Partners have developed Enterprise Information Systems (EIS) that enable corporations to obtain and analyze more easily the data in their corporate computers. Only a few years ago, the software and consulting to build these types of systems cost hundreds of thousands of dollars. Now you can produce the same results with Excel and a few months of macro development.

One of the sizzling show stoppers in EIS systems is the ability to drill-down on a summary item to see the detail that went into that summary item. Excel database reports created with Crosstab Wizard have the drill-down capability built in.

When you are in the last window of the Crosstab Wizard, choose the Set Table Creation Options button. In the Create Options window that appears, select Yes for the option labeled Define Double-Click in the crosstab range to display source data. Choose OK and then choose the Create It button to create your report.

If you want to see the detail information that went into creating a summary item, double-click the item. Excel builds a report on another worksheet that shows you the data that went into that summary item.

If you double-click a quarterly total for the Laser tools product line, for example, Excel builds and displays a worksheet showing you the products in the Laser tools product line and what the sales were within the quarter. This drill-down report is a separate worksheet, so you can change data in it without worrying about changing the original data in the database.

10

Writing Reports

Get the numbers right. Get it out on schedule. And make it look presentable. Any one of these tasks can sometimes be formidable. You expect the numbers and analysis to require thoughtful work, yet sometimes it's the laying out of a report and the presentation that slows you down. The tips in this chapter will help you get your reports done faster, make them look cleaner, and highlight the quality of your numbers.

Use extracts of data for faster reports

You can improve the appearance of detailed reports from your database by using some of the tips that follow. These tips require that you insert columns and copy formulas in your reports. These tasks can create extra work for you if you create reports directly from a database, however; so instead, use an extract or copy of the database to create your reports.

Calculate the rows or columns to hide or display

You can calculate which rows of a report or database to hide with the following trick, which is useful for exception reports, or when the order of records changes or the specifications for the report change.

No matter how the data changes, you can easily rerun the report and hide only the rows that do not meet your specifications. Returning the report to its original form is equally easy, and you can use this same trick to hide columns.

This technique uses a formula that is copied down the side of the database. The formula checks to see which rows *do not* meet the specifications of what you want to display.

Figure 10.1 shows a light machinery database. The selected cells are in the rows that will be hidden. Using this technique, you display only the rows where the sales are greater than the number in cell B8.

The formula results in a #N/A error for rows that should be hidden. You can select all these rows with the Formula Select Special command and then hide them.

The formula in cell A12 is:

```
=IF(H12>$B$8,#N/A,"")
```

This formula matches the Sales in the first database row against the amount typed in cell B8. Because this formula will be copied down the side of the database, you must make B8 an absolute reference so that it doesn't change when copied. The formula results in #N/A when sales are greater than $50,000—the rows that return #N/A are the rows to hide.

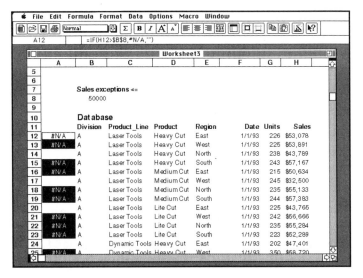

Fig. 10.1 *Selectively hide formulas with the correct formula and two commands.*

Use the following steps to select all the rows to hide:

1. Select column A by clicking the column heading.

2. Choose the Formula Select Special command, and in the Select Special dialog box select the Formulas option.

3. Under the Formulas options, clear all the options except Errors.

4. Choose OK.

   This action selects all the cells that contain #N/A.

5. The selected cells are in the rows you want to hide.

   Hide these rows by choosing the Format Row Height command and then the Hide button.

To return the report to normal so that all rows are displayed, you can repeat the process, but choose the Unhide button in the Row Height dialog box. Alternatively, you can select the entire database and choose the Unhide button.

This technique is a very flexible technique when written with macros. It gives macro programmers all the capabilities of expanding and contracting like the outline feature but is far more flexible.

Calculate subtotals in a list

Many reports are easier to read if you show a subtotal when a category changes. One simple method that doesn't involve macros appears in figure 10.2.

To use this method, you must first sort your database or list on the column by which you are grouping subtotals. Do this sort with the Data Sort command.

In figure 10.2, column H contains running totals that start over when the data changes—forming a subgroup. These running totals by subgroup are produced by entering two formulas.

First, in cell H7, enter the following formula:

=G7

Then, in cell H8, enter the formula

=IF(D8=D7,G8+H7,G8)

This formula tests that the value of cell D8 is equal to the value of D7—the cell above D8. Equal values indicate that the data has not changed in column D; therefore, we should continue to produce a running total of this batch of records.

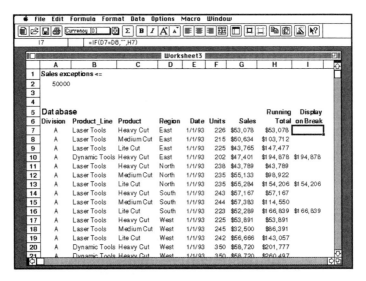

Fig. 10.2 *Create subtotals and totals on breaks using an IF function.*

If D8 equals D7, the total of G8 and G7 is returned in H8—providing you with the running total for this group of records. If D8 does not equal D7, indicating that the data in column D has changed, the value of G8 is returned.

This value becomes the first value of a new group of records and leaves the last running total above as the subtotal for the previous batch of records.

To display subtotals only when the data changes, you need another column. This column—column I in the figure—tests for changes in column D.

The formula in I7 is:

```
=IF(D7=D8,"",H7)
```

Notice that this formula checks the value of cell D7 against the cell below it. If D7 equals D8, the data has not changed and you want to return a blank cell in column I. Therefore, the formula returns " " if this statement proves true.

However, if D7 does not equal D8, you have reached the last cell of a group and want to return the subtotal calculated in column H. Therefore, the formula returns H7 to column I.

If you want only the subtotals in column I to display, hide column H.

Hide repetitive text in lists and reports

Many reports look better if repetitive text does not appear. For example, in figure 10.2 the report might look better if the A's for division appear only at the beginning of the A division, the Heavy Cut appears only at the beginning of the Heavy Cut group, and the East, West, North, and South labels appear only at the start of their groups.

For each column in which you want labels that display when there is a change, you will need to insert a column. In this column, you type another formula similar to the second formula in the preceding tip. You must sort the database or list by the column containing the items by which you are grouping.

Figure 10.3 shows a report where the Region only displays in column E in the first row when a new region begins.

Enter the following formula in cell E7, and then copy it down the length of the database:

=IF(D7<>D6,D7,"")

The formula in cell E7 checks to see whether the region next to it in D7 is the same as the region in the row above. If the regions are different, the adjacent region, D7, is displayed. If the region above is the same, nothing displays. You will not want column D to show its labels, so you can hide column D.

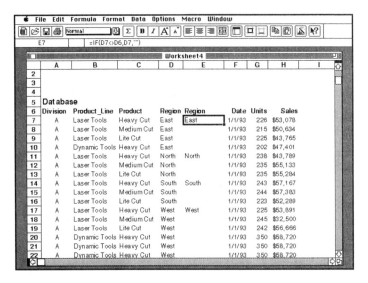

Fig. 10.3 *Use an IF formula to show titles and labels only when they change.*

If you are creating a report that is a summation or cross-tabulation of database information, use the Crosstab ReportWizard. The Crosstab ReportWizard displays subtotals much more elegantly than you can through the use of these formulas. If you need to create reports that show all the detail and not summaries, however, use the formulas in the preceding tips.

Increase line spacing on subtotals

Your reports may look better if you increase the row height for the first row of each record where the category changes.

In figure 10.3, for example, you will probably want the row height to increase in rows 7, 11, 14, and 17. Having extra white space above each group makes the groups easy to distinguish.

To increase the row height at the beginning of each new group of records, enter the formula

=IF(E7<>"",#N/A,"")

in cell I7. Copy this formula down the length of the report. This formula displays the #N/A error in those rows where data appears in column E.

Use the Formula Select Special method described in the earlier tip, "Calculate the rows or columns to hide or display," to select only those cells containing #N/A. After the cells containing #N/A are selected, you can use the Format Row Height command to increase the height of the rows containing the desired data, such as subtotals.

11

Printing and Page Layout

Getting your work to fit on a page or getting the right headers and footers to print is usually the last thing you do. But when you have one eye on the clock and another on the printer, every tip can help. Following are some tips to help you print more effectively.

Print only displayed data from an outline

If you attempt to print an outline that has some levels hidden, you may be surprised and aggravated to find that all levels print.

To print only displayed parts of an outline, you use the Select as Displayed tool, as explained in the following steps:

1. Display the Microsoft Excel 3 toolbar, on which the Select as Displayed tool is to the left of the AutoSum button.

You also can find this tool in the Utility category of the Customize toolbars dialog box, from which you can drag the tool onto any toolbar.

2. Display the outline as you want it, select the area you want to print, and then click the Select as Displayed tool.

3. Choose the Options Set Print Area command.

Then continue with the normal printing process.

Use the View Manager to remember ranges and print settings

The View Manager is an add-in to Excel 4 that remembers ranges, as well as display and print settings. You can assign a name to a view and then return to that exact view at a later time by selecting the name from a list.

Because the View Manager remembers print and display settings for each view, you can assign different view names to different print areas, their hidden rows and columns, and their page setup settings.

To use the View Manager to make your printing easier, perform the following steps:

1. Prepare the worksheet exactly as you want it to print.

   Hide rows or columns that you do not want to print.

2. Select the print range and choose the Options Set Print Area command.

3. If you will also be using the view for other purposes, select any settings from Options Display that you want saved.

4. Choose the File Page Setup command and select the page layout settings that you want the View Manager to save.

5. Choose the Window View command to display the Views dialog box.

6. Choose the Add button to display the Add View dialog box.

7. Type the name you want for the view in the Name edit box.

8. Select the Print Settings check box to save the current print settings along with the view. If you want the hidden rows and columns saved, select the Hidden Rows & Columns check box.

9. Choose OK.

Whenever you want to return to that view and its associated print area, print settings, and hidden rows and columns, choose the Window View command. When the View dialog box appears, select the name of the view you want from the Views list and then choose the Show button. As a shortcut, you can double-click the name in the Views list.

If you did not install the View Manager during the Excel installation, choose the Options Add-ins command and add the View Manager add-in from the Macro Library folder. (Refer to Chapter 1 for more information on using Excel's add-ins.)

Enter multiple-line headers and footers

In Excel 4, you can enter multiple-line headers at the top of each page or footers at the bottom. To enter a multiple-line header or footer, choose the File Page Setup command. In the Page Setup dialog box, choose the Header or Footer button. The Header or Footer dialog box appears.

Type your first header or footer line in the left, center, or right section box. When you want to break the line and move to the next line, press Option+Return. Continue to type until you need another line, and then press Option+Return again.

Use Excel's print preview feature to check that multiple-line headers or footers do not overlap into the body copy area of the page.

Start page numbers at a specific number

If you have a worksheet or chart page from Excel that you need to merge into another document, you need to print the Excel page with the appropriate page number. You can modify a header or footer so that pagination begins with any number you want.

To begin pagination with a specific number, display the Header or Footer dialog box and click the left, center, or right section box. Position the insertion point where you want the page number to appear and click the # icon. This action inserts the code &P, which automatically enters page numbers. To increase or decrease a page number, you add or subtract a number from the &P code.

If you want the first Excel page to print with the page number 31, for example, you modify the code to read

&P+30

Note: Changing the page numbers with this command may have adverse effects on selecting pages to print. Excel can get confused if you add, for instance, 30 numbers to the normal page values and then request a printout of pages 35 through 39.

Show "Page 1 of 12" in headers or footers

Some legal and academic documents must meet certain formatting guidelines. For example, page numbers must appear as "Page 1 of 12," "Page 2 of 12," and so on. Excel can generate this type of page number.

Display the Header or Footer dialog box and click the section where you want the page number. Type **Page**, followed by a space. Click the # icon to insert the &P code. Type another space and the word **of**; follow it with one last space. Finally, click the ++ icon, which inserts the &N code that prints the total page number. Then type the total number.

Your final result should look like the following:

```
Page &P of &N
```

Format headers and footers with different typefaces and sizes

Each section in the Header and Footer windows is like a miniature notepad. You can select and format the text within a section by selecting the text and then clicking the A icon. This action displays a Font dialog box from which you can choose different fonts, sizes, and styles.

Remove all page breaks at one time

To remove all manually entered page breaks, select the entire worksheet and choose the Options Remove Page Break command. (To select the entire worksheet with the mouse, click in the blank square directly to the left of the column headings. To select the entire worksheet with the keyboard, press ⌘+Shift+Spacebar.)

Repeat vertical and horizontal titles on each page

Repeating titles across the top or down the left side of a multiple page printed worksheet can make the printed worksheet easier to use. You need this feature, for example, when you print a database that is more than one page long. The data on the second page is easier to read if the database headings are across the top of the page.

To repeat titles or database headings, select the rows containing the data you want repeated at the top of each page. Click the row numbers to select the entire row, or press Shift+Spacebar. Then choose the Options Set Print Titles command. When the Set Print Titles dialog box appears choose OK.

To repeat row headings down the left column, select the columns you want for left titles. Select columns by clicking on the column headings or by selecting a cell in a column and pressing ⌘+Spacebar. Choose the Options Set Print Titles command. Choose OK when the Set Print Titles dialog box appears.

Set both horizontal and vertical print titles by selecting the rows for the horizontal headings; then hold down the ⌘ key and click the column headings. This action displays a cross on the worksheet of the selected rows and columns. Choose the Options Set Print Titles command and choose OK from the dialog box.

Use any row as print titles

Print titles do not have to appear directly above the columns of data in the report. They can actually appear in any row of the worksheet. After you identify the row(s) as the print titles, Excel matches the columns of print titles row with the rows of data. If the headings above the data do not serve well as print titles, enter a new row below the data and use it as the print titles row.

Leave out the titles when selecting a print area

When you select a print area while using repeating horizontal or vertical titles like those described in the preceding tips, be careful when you set the print area. If the print area overlaps the print titles, you will see two sets of print titles on some of the pages.

To select the correct print area, select the area you want to print, but do not include the rows or columns used in print titles. Choose the Options Set Print Area command.

Check the current print titles or print area

When you choose the Options commands that set the print area or the print titles, you are actually assigning a name to those selections. If you want to see what the current title is or see the current print area, press ⌘+G, select Print_Titles or Print_Areas from the list of names, and choose OK. Excel highlights the current range on the worksheet.

Remove the current print titles or print area

Remove the current print titles or print area by selecting the entire worksheet and choosing the Options Remove Print Titles or Remove Print Area command. You also can locate the name Print_Area or Print_Titles in the Formula Define Name dialog box and press the Delete button.

Visually adjust margins and column widths before printing

What you see in the worksheet may not exactly match the printed effect. Numbers that barely fit in the worksheet cell, for example, may print as ### if they print a little wider than shown in the worksheet.

To see an accurate presentation of printed results and adjust margins or column widths, set your print area and choose the File Print Preview command. When the preview screen displays, click the pointer on the preview or choose the Zoom button. This action shows you an enlarged picture of the image. Click again to return to viewing the entire page.

With the entire page displayed, check for square black handles that mark page margins or column edges. If you do not see the black handles, choose the Margins button. Use the mouse to drag a margin or column edge handle to a new position. You also can zoom in for a closer view and drag margins or column edges. When in the zoomed view, you only see the black handles near the edge of the paper; however, the pointer changes shape to indicate when it is positioned so that you can move a margin or edge.

Be careful when you move margins or column edges. The changes you make change the worksheet and page setup margin settings. When you change the margins on the page you are viewing, you are also changing them on all pages.

Print an enlarged or reduced copy

If your printed worksheet or chart doesn't quite fit on the page, you can enlarge or reduce the print so that it fits. Enlarging or reducing via the File Page Setup command does not affect your worksheet, so you don't have to worry about changing fonts.

To enlarge or reduce a printed result, choose the File Page Setup command. In the Page Setup dialog box, select the Reduce/Enlarge to option button and type the size you want in its edit box. If normal print is a little too large, for example, you may want to try 95%. If you want a print that is a little larger so that it makes a better overhead transparency, try 125%. Reductions below 65% may cause formats to be lost or cell contents to overlap.

This feature is available on most laser printers, but not on some dot-matrix printers.

12

Sorting and Databases

There are two advantages to Excel having flat-file database capability. First, it serves the small nonrelational database needs of many small businesses and corporate departments. Second, it can do analysis and charting of data on its worksheet better than most expensive database packages. That analysis and charting can be done without extensive programming.

For that reason, many companies download data from their corporate computers into Excel and then use Excel to analyze the data. If you're already familiar with Excel's flat-file database capabilities, the tips and tools in this chapter will help you use them even more efficiently.

Sort more than three fields in stages

Although the Sort dialog box shows only three key fields, you can sort as many database columns or fields as you want by sorting the lowest levels first and then working your way up to the highest level.

Suppose, for example, that you want to sort column A as the first key, column B as the second key, column C as the third key, and so on for six keys. If Excel's Sort dialog box handles six keys at one time, you can sort all the columns simultaneously, as follows:

Key	1	2	3	4	5	6
Column	A	B	C	D	E	F

Unfortunately, Excel's Sort dialog box has only three keys, not six. You must, therefore, sort your columns in two stages. The first sort begins with the lowest-level columns, as follows:

Key	1	2	3
Column	D	E	F

The second time through, you sort the higher-level columns, as follows:

Key	1	2	3
Column	A	B	C

Keep your database intact by including blank cells around it

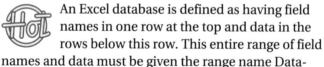 An Excel database is defined as having field names in one row at the top and data in the rows below this row. This entire range of field names and data must be given the range name Database. This name is usually defined by selecting all the cells in the database and choosing the Data Set Database command.

As long as you insert or delete database records (rows) in the middle of this range, the Database name remains intact and usable. Records entered outside the named range will not be included in the database because they are not included in the name. (You can have database "areas" that are not defined with the name Database, but these areas will not be available for searching and extracting procedures.)

If you add data in any rows below the last record in the named range Database, you get into trouble. Excel considers the database to consist only of those cells inside the named range Database. Data added below the named range is not included in Database operations.

You can resolve this problem quickly by setting up your database as an "island," surrounded on all sides by blank cells. If you need a second set of titles above your current database field names, you can leave a blank row above the field names, type the titles above the blank row, and shrink the row height of the blank row to make it disappear.

The blank row is actually still there, but you can't see it. Your database cannot have completely blank records running through it (that is, completely blank rows) that would create a canal, and you would actually have two database islands, not one.

After you set your database (by selecting it and choosing the Data Set Database command), you can rename the database to include any records added at the bottom by using the following procedure:

1. Press ⌘+G to display the Goto dialog box.

2. Select the name Database and choose OK.

3. Choose the Formula Select Special command.

   This command selects all cells touching the active cell. (This is also why you must design the database so that it remains surrounded by a border of blank cells, even as it expands.)

4. Choose the Data Set Database command to redefine Database as the newly selected range.

This procedure can be recorded by using the macro recorder so that you can repeat it by pressing a single shortcut key.

Use OFFSET to create a Sort range for your database

All Excel users seem to sort their databases, but no obvious way exists to do this quickly and easily. You must highlight the data you want to sort and, if your database is like most, the amount of data changes frequently.

You can use the Goto command (⌘+G) to jump to the name Database before sorting, but this includes the field names in the range—which you don't want to sort. How do you quickly select just the data in a constantly-changing database range?

You can enter a formula using OFFSET that calculates the correct range to be sorted. This formula examines the range named Database and uses that range to define a new name, Sort. The Sort range includes all the data in the database, but not the field names.

Enter the following OFFSET formula in the Define Name dialog box:

=OFFSET(Database,1,0,ROWS(Database)-1)

The form for the OFFSET function follows:

`OFFSET(Base_Reference,Rows_Offset,Col_Offset,Height,Width)`

The OFFSET function does not move anything on the worksheet. It merely calculates a new cell or range reference that is based on an existing cell or range reference. In this example, you use the Database range as a Base_Reference from which OFFSET can calculate a Sort range.

The Base_Reference in the function is the current Database. The Rows_Offset value of 1 shifts the calculated reference down one row from where the Database is located. The Col_Offset value of 0 indicates that the Sort is directly in line with the Database range—it is not shifted to the left or right.

The Height of ROWS(Database)-1 calculates the height of the Sort range to be the same height as the Database range, minus one row. One row is left out because the range was shifted down by one to omit the field names. This example has no Width argument, so the width of the new Sort range is the same as the width of the Database.

To create the Sort name, follow these steps:

1. Choose the Formula Define Name command to display the Define Name dialog box.

2. Type the name **Sort** (or any other name you want to use) in the Name edit box.

3. Type the OFFSET formula, as previously shown, into the Refers To edit box.

4. Choose OK.

If you have a defined Database range, you can quickly select its Sort range. If you change the Database range, the Sort range also is recalculated.

To select the Sort range, choose ⌘+G. The name Sort (or the name you typed in the Name edit box) does not appear in the Goto list. Type **Sort** into the Reference edit box, and then choose OK. The Sort range is selected. While the Sort range is selected, you can choose the Data Sort command and not have to worry about sorting field names into the database.

Use absolute references in database formulas that refer to outside cells

If cells in your database contain formulas, make sure that you understand what happens to the formulas when you sort or insert new data. Cell references that refer to other cells in the same record (row) should be *relative references* (those without dollar signs).

Cell references that refer to a cell or range outside the database should be *absolute references* (those with two dollar signs). You can easily create an absolute reference by moving the insertion point next to a cell reference in a formula and then pressing ⌘+T until the reference includes two dollar signs.

If you use relative references in a database to refer to cells outside the database, the references inside the database change incorrectly when you sort the database or insert or delete records.

Use a formula to calculate criteria

Not all the information you want to find in a database is simple. Some of its criteria may need to be calculated. In the database shown in figure 12.1, for example, you may want to find or extract all records in which the product is Heavy Cut and the price per unit is less than $235.

To find those records, you must use a calculation in the Criteria range. Your criteria must calculate the unit price for each Heavy Cut record and then find those records in which the unit price is less than $235.

The trick to using a calculated criteria is to create a new field heading in the Criteria range for the calculated criteria. The field name for that calculated criteria cannot match any field name that heads the database.

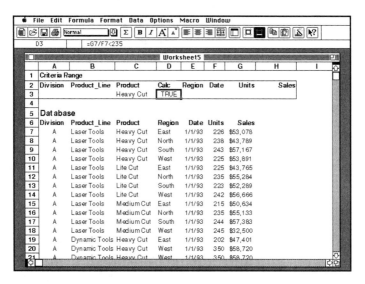

Fig.12.1 *A dummy field name above calculated criteria.*

You must use a made-up (or dummy) field name for calculated criteria. If you put calculated criteria under a valid field name in the Criteria range, it will not work.

The rule for creating a formula for your calculated criteria is that the result of the calculation must be TRUE or FALSE. The cell tested must be in the top row of data. If the first row of data is row 12, for example, and you want to test column B, your formula must test B12.

Calculated criteria that result in TRUE are found or extracted by using a database command. *Dfunctions* (functions that relate to databases, such as DSUM and DAVERAGE) analyze the records that meet calculated criteria resulting in TRUE.

Analyzing records is easiest if you build formulas that test for equalities—is one side equal to the other, is one side

less than the other, and so on. The following table lists
some examples of calculated criteria:

Criteria	Explanation
=D12=G12	Checks for an exact match between data in the same record. Tests TRUE when the cells in column D of a record are the same as the cells in column G of the same record. TRUE results are found or extracted.
=B12=B13	Checks for an exact match between data in two adjacent records. Tests TRUE when two adjacent records have the same data in column B.
=C12<D12/2	Checks for records in which C12 is less than half of D12.
=C12>$B$5	Checks for records in which the data in column C is greater than a number typed in cell B5. B5 is outside the database.

In figure 12.1, the criteria to find records in which the
Product is Heavy Cut and the price per unit is less than
$235 are entered in the Criteria range. Notice that the
heading Calc is used above the calculated criteria. (Any
word could be used above the calculated criteria as long as
the word is not a valid field name.)

Check the Criteria range by selecting it with ⌘+G to make
sure that any calculated criteria heading is within the Criteria range. The calculation used for the criteria in this
example is as follows:

=G7/F7<235

This calculation specifies that the information in
column G, divided by the information in column F,
is less than 235.

Use calculated criteria to find blank cells or filled cells in a database

Use calculated criteria such as those described in the preceding tip when you need to find records that contain a blank cell or find records that contain only filled cells.

In the database and criteria shown in figure 12.1, for example, you can find blank cells in column C by entering the following calculated criteria in cell D3 of the Criteria range:

=C7=""

Notice that this calculation falls under the dummy field heading, Calc. If you want to find records that contain only filled cells in column C, use a calculated criteria such as the following:

=C7<>""

Extract data to another worksheet to make creating reports easier

To create reports from the data in databases, use extracted data formatted on a separate worksheet from that containing the database. Among the advantages to this approach are the following:

■ You can use only one extract range at a time on the worksheet containing the database.

If you extract the data to a separate worksheet, however, you can use multiple worksheets, each with its own Criteria and Extract range.

■ By keeping a single report on each worksheet, you don't need to worry about the row and column formatting from one report interfering with that of another report.

■ You can view multiple extracted reports at the same time by arranging the separate worksheets.

■ Each worksheet that contains an extracted report can be saved as a separate file and transmitted by E-mail or made into a database file itself.

Caution: The following extract procedure assumes that you know how to perform a normal database extract. If not, you may want to review that procedure before attempting any of these steps.

To extract data from a database on one worksheet to an extract range on another worksheet, follow these steps:

1. Create a worksheet containing a database that meets all the Excel database rules.

   Make sure that you name the database by selecting it and choosing the Data Set Database command.

2. Save the database worksheet to a file name that will not change.

3. Create a second worksheet to contain the extract report.

   In this worksheet, you must create a valid Criteria range and Extract range.

   Use the appropriate field names from the Database on the first worksheet.

   Select the Criteria range and choose the Data Set Criteria command.

   Select the Extract headings and choose the Data Set Extract command.

4. You have now created and named a Database on one worksheet and created and named a Criteria and Extract range on a different worksheet.

   Activate the worksheet containing the Extract range.

5. Choose the Formula Define Name command to display the Define Name dialog box.

6. Type the name **Database** in the Name edit box.

7. Type the following formula in the Refers To edit box:

   =*filename*.XLS!Database

   Here, *filename* is the name of the worksheet containing the Database range.

When you are ready to create your report, make sure that both files are open. Then follow these steps:

1. Activate the worksheet containing the Extract range.

2. Enter any criteria in the Criteria range to limit the data extracted.

3. Choose the Data Extract command, and then select the Unique Records Only check box if you want to remove records in which all extracted fields contain the same data.

   You may want to leave the records in to see your entire database history—or remove them to get only one occurrence of each item.

4. Choose OK.

Extracted data that matches your criteria is copied from the worksheet containing the database and is placed below the extract range headings in the second worksheet. You can use the formulas and tips in Chapter 10, "Writing Reports," to format your results.

Use the Extract feature to check for misspelled entries

You can check for misspelled data in your database by performing a *unique extract* (an extract using the Unique Records Only option) on the field you suspect contains misspellings. Your database may, for example, contain 20 different product names under the field name Product. Because the data was entered manually, some of the product names could be misspelled. Misspelled product names invalidate searches, sorts, and analyses.

To check a column for misspelled words, you must create a one-field extract range for the field you want to check and then perform a unique extract. If you have only 20 or 30 valid entries, spotting incorrect entries will be easy.

If you suspect data under the Product heading is misspelled, for example, select a cell that has nothing below it to the bottom of the worksheet. Type the field heading **Product** in that cell. Select the cell, and choose the Data Set Extract command. Then choose the Data Extract command. Select the Unique Records Only check box, and choose OK. The cells below the one containing the heading Product fill with a list containing each unique word in the Product field. The list contains no duplicates.

Look through this list for misspelled product names. If you find a misspelled product name, follow these steps: Locate the misspelling in the database by choosing the Formula Find command and type the misspelling in the Find What edit box. Select the Look in Values option, and choose OK. After you find and correct the misspelling, press the F7 key or ⌘+H to repeat the Find command. This action ensures that no other words with the same misspelling remain in the database.

13

Creating Charts

If you have been an accountant or chief financial officer for 40 years, you can probably scan a page of numbers and pick out some obscure trend. But the rest of us are better served in looking for visual changes, which our hunter-and-gatherer ancestors have been doing for a few hundred thousand years.

Spotting important changes or picking out relationships in financial reports is often much easier when you look at a chart rather than at pages filled with numbers. This chapter provides a number of tips to facilitate your Excel chart work.

Flip the chart's axes by using the ChartWizard

Occasionally, Excel misinterprets its own internal "rules" for converting data into a chart. One such rule involves the orientation of the data—in which directions lie the horizontal and vertical axes? Excel may reverse these axes so that your chart appears to lie on its side.

Excel's automatic charting rule tells it that a *data series* (a line of data in a line chart) is the data that runs the long way—usually horizontally—in the cells you have selected. If you select a range of data that is wider than it is tall, for example, Excel assumes that the data series runs across the row.

A line in a line chart connects all the numbers in the same row. Sometimes, however, the data you select does not run as Excel expects, and the resulting chart appears to be sideways—that is, the data you want on the horizontal axis is on the vertical axis and vice versa.

By using Excel's ChartWizard feature, you can easily fix the errant chart by following these steps:

1. Activate the worksheet that contains the chart's data.

2. Activate the chart.

   If the chart is embedded in the worksheet, double-click the chart.

3. Click the ChartWizard tool at the right side of the Standard toolbar.

   This action displays a ChartWizard dialog box that enables you to select a different range.

4. Choose the Next button.

5. Change the chart orientation by selecting the Data Series in Rows or the Data Series in Columns option button. (Select the *opposite* of the currently selected button.)

   Notice that the sample chart in the ChartWizard dialog box changes to reflect the orientation you selected.

6. Choose OK.

Use chart templates to create frequently drawn charts

If you frequently create the same custom chart but use different data in it, you should consider using chart templates. A *chart template* is a blank chart that stores all the formats and settings for a chart. All you need to do is add data, and the chart redraws itself using the new data.

To create a chart template, follow these steps:

1. Create a chart exactly like those you want to repeat.

   Set the chart's patterns, colors, legend location, fixed titles, axis scaling, page setup settings, and other formatting.

2. Choose the File Save As command.

3. Type an appropriate name for the chart in the File Name edit box, such as **Budget Chart** for those charts you will use for budgeting.

   Using *chart* in the name helps you distinguish between chart templates and worksheet templates.

4. Select the Options button and choose Template from the File Format pull-down list.

5. Choose OK, then select the Excel Startup folder (inside the System folder) as the location for the file, and then choose OK.

When you next start Excel, choose the File New command to see that your chart template is listed among Excel's templates. To create a chart using this template, select the data you want to chart and choose the File New command.

Instead of choosing Chart to open a new chart, however, select the name of your template and choose OK. Excel opens your template, gives it a new name, and displays the selected data in the format defined by the template.

Avoid the Gallery menu to preserve chart formatting when changing chart types

After you have created and customized a chart with colors, patterns, custom scales, and so on, do not attempt to change chart types by choosing the Gallery menu and then selecting another chart type. If you use the Gallery menu to switch from a customized bar chart to a column chart, for example, you may lose some of your custom formatting in the transfer.

To preserve the formatting when you change chart types, choose the Format Main Chart command to display the Format Chart dialog box. Select a new chart type from the Main Chart Type pull-down list. This list displays small samples of the different types of charts available. Select a more specific version of the chart from the Data View group, and then choose OK.

Use the ⌘ key to select a single data point on a chart

If you click on a line, bar, or column, all the markers in that series are selected. Usually that's okay because you normally want to format an entire series the same way. If you want only one line marker, bar, or column (an individual data point) to be in a different color or pattern, however, you must select a single marker, bar, or column.

To select a single marker, hold down the ⌘ key as you click the marker, bar, or column. (Notice that the selection handle appears only on the marker you click.) You also

can click normally on the data series, and then press the
right arrow key until the desired marker is selected.

Separate pie chart segments for extra emphasis

If you want pie chart segments to separate so that a certain segment stands out from the rest, simply click on the
chosen segment and drag it away from the center. As you
drag the wedge out, the pie shrinks in size. Usually, you
don't need to drag a wedge very far to make it stand out.

Create your own line chart symbols

The line chart symbols provided by Excel may be too small
for some charts, especially if you create overhead trans-
parencies. Your industry or company also may have its
own special chart symbols. You can create custom line
chart symbols in MacPaint or any painting or drawing
program, however, and use them for an entire line or a
single data point.

First, create and save your line chart. Then quit Excel and
switch to your graphics program. Draw and color the new
symbol as you want it to appear. After you finish a new
symbol, copy it to the Clipboard by using the graphic
program's Copy command. Then switch back to Excel and
your chart.

To use your symbol for every data point on a line, click the
chart line. To use your symbol to mark a single data point
on a line, use ⌘+click to select only that data point. Then
choose the Edit Paste command. Your symbol replaces the
selected markers on the line.

You also may want to create a file to contain the different
custom symbols you use frequently. That way, if you later

need to create another line chart with a certain symbol, you can copy that symbol from your stored library.

Format the value (vertical) axis by formatting a cell

 The *value axis*, also known as the *Y* or *vertical axis* in two-dimensional charts, takes its format from the first numeric cell of the first data series in the worksheet. To change the numeric format of this axis, simply change the format of that cell using the various formatting commands in the Format menu.

Break legend titles into multiple lines

 If the legends on your chart look awkward because the legend titles are too long, try wrapping the titles to a second line. Unfortunately, however, you cannot enter a line break character in a legend title directly onto the chart. But you can enter a line break into the text of a worksheet cell and then link the legend title to that cell.

To break a legend title into two lines, follow these steps:

1. Select the cell on the worksheet that contains the legend title you want to split.

   This may already be part of the chart.

2. Move the insertion point in the formula bar to the place where you want the legend title to wrap to a new line.

3. Press ⌘+Option+Return to insert a line break in the legend title in the formula bar.

   The actual text inside the cell may not wrap at this time; instead, a black vertical character appears in the cell. (The cell text will wrap if you turn the Wrap

Text alignment option on using the Format
Alignment command.)

4. Press Return to accept your changes.

5. Activate the chart.

   The legend's title appears split on the chart at the
   same point in the text as where you pressed
   ⌘+Option+Return in the worksheet cell.

If you don't want to mar the headings in your worksheet
with the black mark of a line break character—or if you
don't want to split the title on the worksheet by wrapping
the text in that cell, create another split title in a cell in an
unobtrusive part of the worksheet. Activate the chart sheet
and choose the Chart Edit Series command.

In the Edit Series dialog box, select the data series you
want titled, and then clear the Name edit box and place
the cursor in that space. Activate the worksheet containing the alternative title, and select the cell containing that
title (which, by the way, should include the wrapped lines
as described above). Choose OK to accept the new name
for that data series in the chart.

Link worksheet numbers or text to your chart's floating text

Charts often are more informative if they show dates,
numbers, titles, or comments that are linked to cells on
the worksheet. Linking chart text to worksheet cells enables you to show the current date in a chart or incorpo-
rate a text comment from a worksheet cell as a floating
text block. As the dates, numbers, titles, or comments in
the worksheet change, they also change in the chart.

To link a floating text block in a chart to data in a
worksheet cell, follow these steps:

1. Click a blank area of the chart so that no text is selected.

2. Type an equal sign (=).

3. Activate the worksheet containing the cell you want to link by clicking the worksheet or by choosing it from the Window menu.

4. Click the cell that contains the data you want in the chart.

5. Press Return.

The chart is reactivated and shows the contents of the worksheet cell in a floating text box. The text box appears approximately where you typed the equal sign. You can format this text block just as you can format any floating text.

What you have created by using this procedure is an external reference formula to the worksheet cell, which is similar to the formulas used to link worksheet cells. You can see this by selecting the floating text that is linked to the worksheet cell and by looking at the external reference displayed in the formula bar.

Use the ChartWizard to expand the charted data

If the data plotted by your chart has expanded to include additional worksheet cells, you don't need to draw a new chart. You can use the ChartWizard to extend the chart's data range.

Follow these steps to extend the data range by using the ChartWizard:

1. Activate the worksheet containing the data.

2. Activate the chart. (Double-click on the chart to activate it if it is embedded.)

3. Click the ChartWizard tool at the far right of the Standard toolbar.

   The first Wizard dialog box appears. The edit box in this window enables you to edit the ranges used by charts.

4. Edit the range currently listed in the Range edit box, or enter a new data range by selecting the cell reference you want to change and then dragging to highlight the new range in the worksheet.

5. Choose the Next button.

6. Choose OK.

You have now changed the previous data range for the chart—or updated it to include additional data. The ChartWizard is the easiest way to modify existing data ranges.

Use named data ranges to expand or contract charts easily

Many sales and budget worksheets require that you add new data for each month to the end of existing data. A chart of the worksheet, however, does not automatically expand to include new data. When you create the chart, you can leave room for the entire worksheet range, including data to be added later. If you plan for twelve months of data, however, your chart will contain several months of blank space throughout most of the year.

An alternative is to edit the chart's series formulas to include the additional cells as you fill them. You can use the Chart Edit Series command or click the ChartWizard to reselect or extend the range of cells charted, but doing so is tedious, error prone, and time-consuming, especially over a 12-month period.

A better solution is to edit your chart so that it searches for its data in named ranges on the worksheet. If you change the definition of the named range, the chart expands or contracts to include the data in the new name.

Figure 13.1 shows a worksheet containing data through April for the data series Revenue and Cost. Notice that cell A3 contains a text title that is normally not present, X_Titles. This title is used later to more easily create names. You can hide it for now by formatting its font color or by using the Format Number command and entering the numeric custom number format of four semicolons: ;;;;.

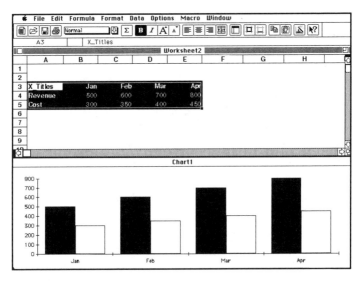

Fig. 13.1 *Labels (in cells A3:A5) used to name data ranges for the chart.*

To re-create this example, type the data as shown, and then highlight the data range and choose File New to create a new chart from the data. Use the Window Arrange command to arrange the windows horizontally.

To see that the chart is not automatically updated, type the title **May** in the worksheet and add May Revenue and Cost numbers. Notice that the chart does not reflect the appended data. Erase the May title and data.

To edit the chart so that it expands to include monthly data appended at the end of the worksheet, you must create new names on the worksheet and then edit these names into the chart's series formulas.

First, on the worksheet create the names that describe where the data and the Category (X-axis) labels are located by following these steps:

1. Select cells A3:E5.

    Notice that cells A3, A4, and A5 each contain text that can be used as a name to identify the data to the right. The command that follows uses the text in the far-left cell to assign a name to the data cells to the right.

2. Choose the Formula Create Names command to display the Create Names dialog box.

3. Select the Left Column check box.

    Make sure that all other check boxes are deselected.

4. Choose OK.

You can check whether the three names for the cells from B3:E5 have been created correctly by pressing the Goto key (F5). Select the X_Labels, Revenue, or Cost name from the list, and choose OK. The labels or data in cells B3:E5 should be selected. The text in column A will not be included.

Now you must use the Edit Series command to edit the chart's series formulas so that the chart searches for named ranges rather than for specific cell references.

To edit the chart's series formulas, follow these steps:

1. Activate the chart.

2. Choose the Chart Edit Series command to display
the Edit Series dialog box.

   Figure 13.2 shows this dialog box with the Revenue
   data series selected. Notice that the edit boxes list
   the cells used to retrieve a series name (legend), X
   labels (horizontal axis), and Y values (vertical axis).

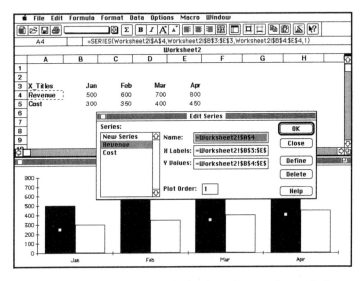

Fig. 13.2   *The Edit Series dialog box, listing the worksheet
cells referenced by the chart.*

3. Select the first data series, Revenue, from the Series
list box.

   The edit boxes on the right list the cells referred to by
   this series.

4. Edit the X Labels edit box so that it uses the range
name **X_Titles** instead of $B$3:$E$3.

5. Edit the Y Values edit box so it uses the range name **Revenue** instead of $B$4:$E$4.

6. Choose the Define button. The edited Revenue series should appear as shown in figure 13.3.

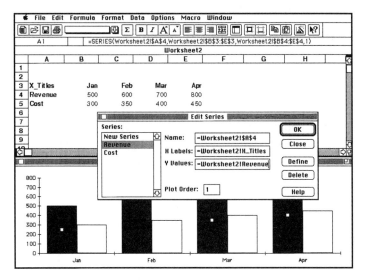

Fig. 13.3 *The cell references replaced by named ranges on the worksheet.*

7. Repeat steps 3 through 6 for the Cost series. In step 5, use the range name **Cost** to replace $B$5:$E$5.

8. Choose OK.

9. Save your chart.

The chart now looks to named ranges on the worksheet for its data. If the named ranges are redefined to include more or less data, the chart adjusts accordingly.

To see exactly how the chart adjusts, follow these steps:

1. Add a title and data for the month of May in cells F3:F5.

2. Reselect the range that includes all chart data (now A3:F5).

3. Choose the Formula Create Names command, and select only the Left Column check box.

   Deselect all other check boxes.

4. Choose OK.

   You are prompted whether you want to redefine each of the names.

   Choose the Yes button each time.

After all the names are redefined, the chart redraws itself to include the new data defined by the new range names. To make this process even easier, you can update the data and rename the chart data by using a recorded macro.

Use named formulas to create charts that adjust to changing amounts of data

By using named formulas, you can create charts that adjust themselves when you append a new month of data. You don't even need to redefine the range names; formulas recalculate the definitions of the range names and perform all the work behind the scenes—without even the use of a macro.

Note: This technique works only with Excel 4 or newer versions.

To use this technique, you must first go through the process described in the preceding tip. You must replace the chart's X labels and Y values references in the Edit Series dialog box with names that refer to the worksheet.

This actions create names in the worksheet that are formulas. These formulas calculate the cell or range reference that defines the named range. If you change the size of a data series by appending a new month's data or removing a month, the formula recalculates and produces a new reference for the range.

To use named formulas in your charts, follow these steps:

1. Create the worksheet and chart as described in the preceding tip.

   The chart must reference the names in the worksheet.

2. Activate the worksheet.

3. Choose the Formula Define Name command to display the Define Name dialog box.

4. Select one of the names referenced by the chart—for example, Revenue.

5. Select the Refers To edit box.

   Press ⌘+U or F2 to edit the box without changing the references.

   Notice that after you press F2, the Status bar changes from Enter to Edit.

6. Enter the following formulas in the Refers To edit box for each of the range names used by the chart.

Name	Formula to enter in Refers To edit box
X_Titles	=OFFSET($B$3,0,0,1,COUNTA($B$3:$M$3))
Revenue	=OFFSET($B$4,0,0,1,COUNTA($B$4:$M$4))
Cost	=OFFSET($B$5,0,0,1,COUNTA($B$5:$M$5))

7. After you finish entering a formula for all the names, choose OK.

You have just created three named formulas. In this example, the OFFSET functions calculate a range that defines each name. Data that is typed into the first blank cell at the end of a row of existing data increases the COUNTA result by one. This action increases the width of the named range by one cell.

The form for the OFFSET function is as follows:

`OFFSET(base_point,row_offset,col_offset,height,width)`

In the Revenue example, the base point—where the Revenue range begins—is $B$4. The starting point is not offset by any rows or columns from the $B$4 point, so the `row_offset` and the `col_offset` values are both `0`.

The `height` of the data range you are defining is one cell high. The `width` is defined by how many *adjacent* cells are filled between $B$4 and the last cell for the last month, $M$4.

You must know one last thing before you can start adding data to the end of a series. The range names and the chart do not always recognize that you have appended data to the end of the series.

The chart, therefore, may not always be updated when you type new data at the end of the series. You can fix this problem manually by changing one of the numbers inside the data series of the chart. This action forces the chart to reexamine its worksheet references so that the chart updates and includes the new data.

If you want the chart updated automatically, type =**NOW**() in any blank worksheet cell. This NOW function produces the current date and time. You then must link the chart to the cell that contains the NOW function by activating the chart, clicking a blank area in the chart, and typing an equal sign (=) to start a formula in the formula bar of the chart.

Activate the worksheet and click on the cell containing the NOW function. Then press Return. Because NOW is always changing, the chart continually reevaluates its references and, in the process, recalculates the names defined by the OFFSET formulas. To prevent the date from the NOW function from appearing in the chart, format it with the same color as the chart's background so that it can't be seen.

Retitle legends by using the Edit Series command

If you create legends for your chart by using the ChartWizard or by choosing the Chart Add Legend command, Excel uses the labels from each data series to create the titles for these legends. You can change the legends Excel has selected if your chart does not have labels for a legend.

To change the titles used in legends on your chart, choose the Chart Edit Series command to display the Edit Series dialog box. Select from the Series list the name of the data series with the title you want to change. The Name edit box displays the cell from which the legend takes its title in this data series.

Select the Name edit box. To link the legend title for that data series to a different worksheet cell, choose the Window menu and then select the worksheet that contains the cell with the new legend title. Scroll to and select the cell containing the new title. The external reference to that new title appears in the Name edit box.

If you want to type a new legend title instead of using one in a worksheet cell, select the Name edit box. Clear the edit box and type the title that you want. Choose OK. This new title does not change if you change the label for the data in the worksheet.

Use the color palette to change colors in 3-D surface maps

The colors used in 3-D surface maps come from the color palette. They cannot be changed by formatting as can colors or patterns in other charts.

To change the colors in a 3-D surface map, follow these steps:

1. Activate the worksheet from which the chart was created.

2. Choose the Options Color Palette command, and select the color you want to change from those colors in the Color Palette box.

3. Choose the Edit button to display the Color Picker window.

4. Select a custom color from this window, and then choose OK.

   The custom color you select replaces the original color in the Color Palette box.

   This color also replaces that color throughout the worksheet as well as in the chart.

5. Choose the OK button to accept this new color palette.

Create a chart with two different axis scales

You may find it necessary to add a second Y-axis to your chart. This addition will give you an axis on the left and another on the right. You can do this for any combination chart by choosing the Gallery Combination command. From the Chart Gallery dialog box, select the two-axis chart that is closest to the chart you want, and choose OK.

If you want to change the type of chart used by the master chart—the one with the left axis—choose the Format Main Chart command and select a new chart type from the Main Chart Type pull-down list. Then select a specific chart from the Data View group.

To change the type of chart used by the right axis, choose the Format Overlay command. Select a new chart type from the Main Chart Type pull-down list, and then select a specific chart from the Data View group.

14

CHAPTER

Working with Multiple Worksheets

Excel lets you open and work with several worksheets and windows at the same time. But you pay a price for that flexibility. These tips help you work with multiple documents and keep your computerized desktop clean.

Use keyboard shortcuts to move between windows

When working with multiple windows (worksheets) at the same time, use the following shortcuts:

Shortcut Keys	Action
⌘+F6	Move to the next window
⌘+Shift+F6	Move back through the windows
⌘+F4	Close the active window
⌘+F10	Maximize the active window

Move a window without activating it

You can move a window without bringing it to the front. Just press and hold the ⌘ key as you drag the window's title bar. The window remains behind the others as you move it.

Open new windows on the same worksheet for separate views

If you need to see two widely separated areas of the same worksheet at the same time—for example, the result area and the data entry—open two windows onto the same worksheet.

Open a second window onto the active worksheet by choosing the Window New Window command. You can format and move each window independently, and each window can have its own Options Display settings.

Be careful when you save or close while using multiple windows that show the same worksheet. If you use the File Close command, for instance, you close the file—which is all the windows.

To close the active window but leave other windows on the worksheet open, click the Close box in the upper-left corner of the unwanted window.

If you save a worksheet while multiple windows are open, the next time you open the worksheet all the same windows appear.

Freeze window panes to keep titles in sight

If you work in a large worksheet or database, you probably lose sight of row or column headings as you scroll through the worksheet. The way to keep those headings in sight is to split the window into frozen panes.

To freeze a horizontal pane and keep top heading rows in sight, complete the following steps:

1. Scroll the headings so that they are in the top rows of the screen.

2. In the far-left column of the screen, select the cell under the headings' lowest row.

3. Choose Window Freeze Panes.

   A horizontal line appears above the selected cell. You cannot scroll the headings away now.

To freeze a vertical pane and keep left-side columns of headings in sight, complete the following steps:

1. Scroll the headings so that they are against the left edge of the screen.

2. In the top row of the screen, select the cell to the right of the last heading column.

3. Choose Window Freeze Panes.

   A vertical line appears to the right of the headings. You cannot scroll these headings away now.

To remove the frozen pane, choose the Window Unfreeze Pane command.

Split a window quickly and freeze panes

If you use the Window Freeze Panes command before you split a window into panes, the command splits the window and freezes panes for you—in one step. Move the cell pointer to the cell marking the intersection of the row and column you want to freeze (and split), and then choose Window Freeze Panes.

15

Creating Macros

Both novices and application developers can use Excel's macro language. The novice can record and modify macros, and the application developer can use Excel's programming language, which contains more than 1,000 functions.

Understand the concept behind Excel macros

Excel macros involve a concept different from other macros or programming languages. If you understand that concept, you will find macros much easier.

In Excel worksheets, you see the results of formulas. The formulas that produce those results are *behind* the results. If you choose the Options Display command and check the Formulas option, the underlying formulas on the worksheet appear.

Excel macros operate in much the same way as the worksheet, but the macro functions and formulas display and their results are hidden underneath. If you display a macro sheet, and then remove the check from the Formulas option in the Options Display command, the results produced by macro functions display. These results may appear as TRUE, FALSE, an error value, or as a calculated or entered result that is a number or text.

Most functions produce a value of TRUE when they operate correctly. When functions operate but fail to produce a result, functions result in a FALSE. For example, if you choose the Cancel button in a dialog box displayed by a function, a FALSE in that function's cell results. Formulas that calculate results, or functions that request data, such as the INPUT function, produce the formula's answer, or the data typed into the Input dialog box.

If you know the result you want in a cell, use IF functions in the macro to change the macro based upon the TRUE and FALSE results from other functions. Reference the numeric or text results in a macro functions cell the same way you use worksheet references in worksheet formulas.

Type macro functions, references, and names in lowercase

Excel macro sheets and worksheets check cell references, functions, and names when you enter them. If the references, functions, or names are valid, Excel capitalizes them on entry. Function names and references are capitalized on entry. Range names match the way they were typed when you entered them. For this reason, create range names with the first letter capitalized.

If a function, cell reference, or range name does not change its capitalization when you enter it and press Return, this indicates that Excel does not recognize it as valid.

Disable STEP functions while keeping them available for later troubleshooting

If you want to examine any section of macro code, the STEP function is a handy function to insert before that code. The macro runs normally until it reaches the STEP function. From that point, the macro runs in Step mode. In Step mode, you can choose the Evaluate button to see the partial and full results from a function, or choose the Continue button to return to normal run mode.

After your macro finishes, you may want to remove the STEP functions—they get in the way of normal operation. But don't clear them. Instead, deactivate them and keep them in the macro. If you later need to troubleshoot the macro, reactivate the STEP functions you used when you developed the macro.

To deactivate the operational STEP functions, perform the following steps:

1. Select the areas that contain STEPs you want to deactivate.

2. Choose the Formula Replace command.

3. Type =**STEP** in the Find What edit box.

4. Type **STEP** in the Replace With edit box.

5. Choose the Replace All button.

   This replaces all the =STEP with STEP.

   Without the = sign, the STEP entry is simply text, and is not evaluated by the macro.

Display dialog boxes in recorded macros

When you replay a recorded macro, the dialog boxes in which you made selections never appear. During playback of the macro, you never get a chance to change the options in the dialog boxes. You can easily make the dialog boxes display so that you can select new options during the macro playback.

To display any recorded dialog box, first find the macro function for that dialog box. These functions are usually fairly obvious—for example, FORMAT.FONT displays the Font dialog box and ALIGNMENT displays the text Alignment dialog box. To make the dialog box appear, type a question mark in front of the first parenthesis, as in the following example:

```
=ALIGNMENT?(1,FALSE,3,0)
```

When you run the macro, the Alignment dialog box appears and waits for you to choose the OK button. When you record the macro, the dialog box options you select are stored as the arguments of the function and are used as the default settings for the dialog box when it appears.

Use the FORMULA(INPUT( )) combination for simple data entry

Many people want to use macros for data entry. Here is one of the easiest ways to make a simple data entry macro that prompts the operator, checks the type of data (text or number), and enters the data in the correct cell.

With your worksheet active, follow these steps:

1. Choose the Macro Record command.

   When the Record Macro dialog appears, type a name for the macro.

Do not use spaces, and enter a shortcut key if you want one.

Choose OK.

2. Choose the Macro menu.

   If the command Relative Record is available, press Esc or ⌘+. (period). This cancels the procedure.

   If the Absolute Record command is available, choose it.

   Choosing Absolute Record records the absolute cell locations in which you want to enter data. The macro works on playback, no matter which cell you start it from.

3. Select the first cell in which you want to enter data.

4. Type a description of the data that goes in the cell, and then press Return.

   This description records in the macro and helps you identify which cell the macro is entering data into.

5. Repeat Steps 3 and 4 for each cell and description.

   Select the cells in the order in which you want the operator to enter the data. If you make a mistake, just continue—you can edit the mistake out of the macro sheet.

6. Choose the Macro Stop Recorder command.

You have created a macro that selected each data entry cell, and entered a description in that cell. If you choose the Macro Run command, select the name of your macro, and choose OK, you see the macro repeat your selections and entries.

Modify your data-entry macro to prompt for user input

To modify your macro so that it prompts an operator for the data to enter, follow these steps:

1. Choose the Window command and activate the macro sheet that contains the macro you named.

    The macro's name appears in row 1.

    The macro code appears as SELECT functions that select cells using the row and column number, and also as FORMULA functions that enter the description in the selected cell.

    You modify the FORMULA function so that it displays a dialog box that prompts the operator for an entry.

    The macro code looks similar to the following:

    ```
    =SELECT("R3C3")
    =FORMULA("Amount")
    ```

2. Select the quoted text inside the FORMULA function and choose the Formula Paste Function command to display the Paste Function dialog box.

3. Select the function INPUT from the Paste Function list.

    Make sure that the Paste Arguments check box is selected, and then choose OK.

    The FORMULA function cell now looks like the following:

    ```
    =FORMULA(INPUT(message_text,type_num,title_text,
                   default,x_pos,y_pos,help_ref))
    ```

4. Replace the message_text with a message that prompts the operator. Type your message in quotes.

That message appears in the dialog box, prompting the user to enter data.

5. If you want to restrict entries to numbers or dates, replace type_num with a **1**; if entries can be text, numbers, or dates, replace with a **2**.

6. Replace title_text with the title that you want to appear at the top of the dialog box. Type the title in quotes.

7. Replace default with any number or text that you want the operator to use as the standard entry.

   If the type_num is **2** (text), you must enclose your text default in quotes.

8. Delete the x_pos, y_pos, and help_ref arguments.

9. Press Return.

Your FORMULA(INPUT()) combination may appear similar to the following:

```
=FORMULA(INPUT("Type the amount.",1,"Expense
               Entry",20))
```

Repeat this process for a few FORMULA functions. Then *activate the appropriate worksheet* and run your macro. If it does not run, check to make sure that there are matching quotes and matching parentheses.

There should be no spaces outside of quoted text. Make sure that the commas are in the correct locations and are not periods. Make sure that the worksheet is active when you run this macro, or it may enter data over the top of the macro code.

Transfer data with FORMULA() and COPY()

In Excel 3, macro programmers were accustomed to transferring blocks of data by copying from one worksheet, activating another worksheet, and pasting into that sheet. This process was slow because the programmer had to activate worksheets; also, the process used the Clipboard. Also, some programmers built a FOR-NEXT or FOR-CELL loop that went through every cell in the block and, using the FORMULA function, transferred the cells one at a time.

In most cases, the second method was faster because the receiving worksheet did not need to be activated. The second method also enabled the macro to calculate or manipulate the data as it transferred. (See the tip "Calculating data being transferred.")

In Excel 4, you can transfer blocks of data rapidly—and neither the source nor target worksheets needs to be active. But both worksheets do need to be open. Use the COPY function—its form is as follows:

```
COPY(from_reference,to_reference)
```

The `from_reference` and `to_reference` must meet the same cell size and shape conditions you use when you manually copy and paste.

Note: The references must include the worksheet name if the worksheet is not active. If you need to do calculations with the data in the `from_reference` as it is being transferred, you should still use a loop and the FORMULA function as described in the following tip.

Calculate data as it transfers by using FORMULA

The FORMULA function is used to transfer data from one location to another. Its form is as follows:

```
FORMULA(reference_from,reference_to)
```

If the `reference_to` argument is not specified, FORMULA places the values from the `reference_from` argument into the active cell. Most macro programmers use FORMULA by specifying a `from` location and a `to` location to transfer data between open worksheets as in the following example:

```
=FORMULA(BUDGET!$A$6,SUMMARY!June)
```

This transfers the amount from $A$6 in the BUDGET worksheet into the cell named `June` in the SUMMARY worksheet. You can do more than simply transfer data, however. You also can perform mathematical calculations during the transfer, as shown in the following examples:

```
=FORMULA(BUDGET!$A$6*9,SUMMARY!June)
```

```
=FORMULA(JUNE!Amount+JULY!Amount,SUMMARY!Total)
```

The first example multiplies the value from $A$6 times 9 and then transfers the result to the second worksheet. The second example adds together the numbers stored under the name `Amount` in two different worksheets and then transfers the sum into the cell named `Total` on the SUM-MARY worksheet.

Convert graphic objects or drawings into buttons to run macros

You can convert any graphic object or drawing into a button that runs a macro. To assign a macro to a graphic, drawing, or even an embedded chart, perform the following steps:

1. Open the macro sheet that contains the macro you want to run.

   If the macro sheet is in the current directory, you don't have to open it.

2. Select the graphic, drawing, or chart.

   Black handles appear at the object's corners when it is selected.

3. Choose the Macro Assign to Object command to display the Assign to Object dialog box, and select the macro you want to run from the Assign Macro list.

4. Choose OK, and then select a cell so that the object is no longer selected.

Clicking on the graphic object now runs the macro assigned to it. If you need to see which macro is assigned to a particular graphic "button," press the ⌘ key as you click the button, and then choose the Macro Assign to Object command. The name of the assigned macro appears in the Reference edit box.

Select customized buttons by using ⌘+click

After you draw a graphic and assign a macro to it, you may need to move or reformat the graphic. Every time you click the graphic to select it for formatting, however, the graphic runs the macro assigned to it. To select a graphic or button assigned a macro without running the macro, hold down the ⌘ key as you click the graphic or button.

Split windows to freeze buttons in view on a pane

You may find that your macro buttons move off-screen when you scroll the window of your worksheet. To prevent this, place your buttons along the top or left side of the worksheet. Select the cell directly below the row of buttons and to the right of the column(s) of buttons. Choose the Window Freeze Pane command. This freezes the top rows and left columns of the worksheet. The top row stays in place as you scroll up or down, and the left column(s) stays in place as you scroll left or right.

Assign your macros to tools

To access your favorite macros quickly, add them to a toolbar. Follow these steps to assign a macro to a tool on the toolbar:

1. Open the macro sheet that contains the macro you want to add to the toolbar.

2. Display the toolbar to which you want to add your custom tool by choosing its name with the Options Toolbars command.

3. Choose the Options Toolbars command.

   After the Toolbars dialog box appears, choose the Customize button.

4. Select Custom from the Categories list.

5. Drag one of the custom toolfaces from the Customize dialog box onto a toolbar and drop it there.

   The Assign to Tool dialog box appears.

6. From the Assign to Tool dialog box, select the macro you want to run when this tool is clicked, and choose OK.

7. Choose Close.

The macro sheet containing the macros you have assigned to tools must be open for your custom tool to work. To ensure that a macro sheet is open whenever you run Excel, copy the macro sheet into the Excel Startup folder in the System folder.

Assign a macro to an existing tool

Most tools shown in the Categories list of the Customize dialog box already have functions assigned to them. You can, however, assign a macro to any tool on any toolbar. Your macro then takes precedence over the normal action of that tool.

To assign a macro to a tool, open the macro sheet (or sheets) containing the macros you want to assign. Display the Customize dialog box, and then click the tool to which you want to assign a macro. Choose the Macro Assign to Tool command. After the Assign to Tool dialog box appears, select the macro you want this tool to run when clicked, and then choose OK.

Make the first item you want selected the default item in a custom dialog box

When you create a dialog box by using the Dialog Editor, keep in mind that the first selectable item you create is considered by Excel to be the default item in that dialog box. The default item is always the item selected when the dialog box appears. For greatest efficiency, therefore, make sure that the default item is always the one you want to work with first when accessing the custom dialog box— whether to type in an edit box or scroll through a list box.

This first item is also the first selectable item as you go down the rows in the dialog description table on a macro sheet. A text item may precede an edit box in the description table, for example, but the edit box is still the first selectable item.

What often throws off this simple rule is that the OK and Cancel buttons are always designated as the default item in a dialog box containing either or both these items. When you originally add an OK or a Cancel button to a dialog box by using the Dialog Editor, that button becomes the default button.

Default OK or Cancel buttons take precedence over the first selectable item in the dialog description table. If you add an OK or Cancel button to a dialog box by choosing the Item Button command, therefore, you must deselect the Default check box in the Item Button dialog box.

Create moveable dialog boxes that include titles

Custom dialog boxes are friendlier and more informative when the user can drag them to a different location on-screen and when they show a descriptive title. You can accomplish both tasks while you are in the dialog editor. Double-click the background of the dialog box so that the Dialog Info dialog box appears. In the Text box, type the title you want at the top of your dialog box. Dialog boxes that have a title are moveable.

If you have already created a dialog box and pasted it into a dialog description table on your macro screen, you can still add a title and make it moveable. Enter your title in the text column in the first row of the table. In other words, enter the title into the sixth column of the first row. The first row describes the dialog box size. The sixth column contains text descriptions or displays.

Enter some functions as arrays to use them correctly

Functions such as FILES, DIRECTORIES, DOCUMENTS, and WINDOWS are array functions. These functions return an horizontal array of results. You can retrieve individual items from within these arrays with an INDEX function. INDEX(FILES,1,5), for example, retrieves the name of the fifth file in the FILES array.

Dealing with these arrays is not always straightforward. In some cases you need to transpose the horizontal array into a vertical array. After the array is vertical, you can use its contents in a scrolling list of a custom dialog box.

Figure 15.1 shows a macro sheet in two windows that uses DOCUMENTS to read all the open documents so that they can be displayed in a list in a custom dialog box. Choosing one of these document names from the list activates it. Getting the horizontal array transposed and into a vertical array is the part that requires a trick.

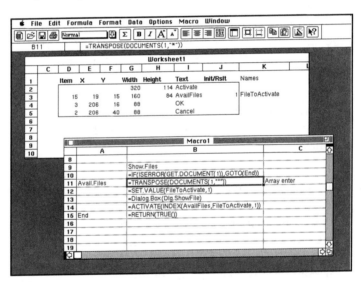

Fig. 15.1   *Load arrays directly into scrolling list boxes.*

You need a description of the code and dialog box first. Beginning with the upper window, the dialog box is defined as Dlg.ShowFile in the range E2:K5. K3 is the cell containing the number of the item selected from the list. This cell is named FileToActivate. If the third item in the list is chosen, K3 and FileToActivate are 3.

The lower window contains the macro that displays the dialog box described by the range Dlg.ShowFile. The names in column A, Avail.Files and End, name the cells to the right in column B. The formula in cell B10 sends the macro to the End if no document is open.

Here is the part that isn't in the manuals: The TRANSPOSE function in cell B11 transposes the horizontal array returned by DOCUMENTS. But only the first document named is usable by the Avail.Files name unless you enter the TRANSPOSE(DOCUMENTS()) formula as an array. *You must enter it by pressing ⌘+Enter.*

Notice the braces {} in the formula bar that indicate an array formula. This vertical list that passes from the TRANSPOSE array into Avail.Files can now be used in cell J3 as the contents for the scrolling list box.

The SET.VALUE function sets the first choice in the list as the default. The INDEX function selects the document from the vertical Avail.Files list, and that document is activated by ACTIVATE.

Use INDIRECT to work with calculated range names

If you try to enter text into a dialog box when Excel is expecting a cell or range reference, your macro halts. Figure 15.2 shows one way to handle this. In the example, a worksheet named NAMEDSHT contains columns named with the Formula Define Name command. The purpose of the macro is to activate the worksheet and then start at the top and select in turn the columns named Col1, Col2, and Col3.

This macro is actually useful for selecting a named set of columns or rows, hiding the selected columns and rows, and then printing a report. Those hidden columns and rows then redisplay, and the next set in the list is used for the next report.

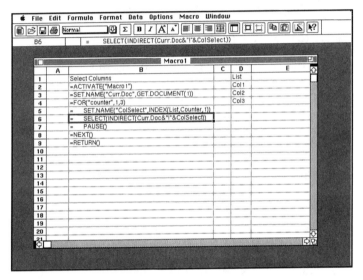

Fig. 15.2 *Use INDIRECT to convert text names and references to valid references.*

The macro begins by insuring that the worksheet with the named columns is active. Cell B3 then stores the name of the active document in the name Curr.Doc. By using a variable name for the active document, you can use this macro with different active documents.

The FOR-NEXT loop in cells B4 and B8 loops through the list three times so that each column name is used. The SET.NAME stores the name for that pass through the loop. *But the name is stored in SET.NAME as text*, which can cause a problem because the SELECT function in cell B6 expects to work on a reference, not text.

The INDIRECT function converts a full reference in text form into a valid reference. Because a full reference is needed, the function concatenates the document name, an exclamation mark, and the name of the column together. Each time through the loop the column name is different, so a different column or columns are selected.

The PAUSE function pauses the macro after each pass through the loop so that you can see what was selected. If you duplicate this macro, click the Resume tool to resume the macro when it is paused.

You also may want to investigate the TEXTREF and REFTEXT functions for some types of conversions between text and references.

Create scrolling lists that allow multiple selections

Some types of scrolling lists just beg the user to make multiple selections at one time—for example, selecting multiple reports to print, selecting multiple files to download from the mainframe, selecting multiple product names to be entered in a table, and so on. Why keep going back to the well when you can install a pipeline?

The dialog box and macro in figure 15.3 show you how to enable multiple selections in a scrolling list and how to handle the multiple selections the user makes. The dialog box description table is named Dlg.City and is in the range A3:G6.

The list that appears in the dialog box is named List.Cities and is in range F9:F18. You load the list of cities into the scrolling list by putting the name of the list in cell F4, which is the text column for the scrolling list.

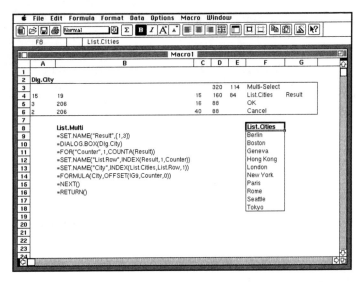

Fig. 15.3 *Give your users the chance to make multiple selections.*

The scrolling list allows multiple selections because cell G4, the Init/Result cell for the list, contains a name— Result. Normally the row number of the selected list item is put in the Init/Result cell for a scrolling list. But *if there is a name in this cell, Excel allows multiple selections from the list.* (You can use any valid name. It does not have to be Result.)

Cell B9 shows you how to set a default for the multiple selection list. Simply enter numbers into the range specified by the name (in this case Result). These numbers indicate which items in the list are selected by default. *Notice the braces typed around the 1,3.* This is one of the few times you can use braces. You *do not* have to enter this as an array by pressing ⌘+Enter.

After the dialog box appears, you can hold down the ⌘ key and click multiple selections in the list. When you choose OK, Excel stores, in Result, the numbers of all the rows you selected. The rest of the macro uses the resulting selections to pull items from the list of cities and enter them into the worksheet.

16

Creating Custom Applications

When you become proficient with macros, you may want to try building a *custom interface* for your worksheet applications. A custom interface involves custom menus, dialog boxes, and other techniques that enhance a worksheet for others to use.

Create toggle buttons

You can often replace two buttons with one toggle button. A toggle button switches between two different functions and is useful for on/off actions. For example, you may want to use a toggle button to display and then hide a chart on a worksheet. When the chart is visible, the button says Hide Chart. When it is hidden, the button says Display Chart.

To create a toggle button, start with separate buttons for each function. Create and attach the appropriate macro to each button; then add the following macro lines at the beginning of each button's macro.

Add these lines to the beginning of the first button's macro:

```
=SELECT("BUTTON2")
=BRING.TO.FRONT()
=SELECT()
```

Add these lines to the beginning of the second button's macro:

```
=SELECT("BUTTON1")
=BRING.TO.FRONT()
=SELECT()
```

Note: Be sure to use the actual names of the buttons in place of `"BUTTON1"` and `"BUTTON2"` in this example. To determine the button's number, select the button and look at the upper-left corner of the screen at the active cell indicator on the formula bar. The point is that each button's macro activates the other button.

Now, place one button on top of the other and adjust them so that they completely overlap each other. They must be the same size and shape.

Protect worksheets with buttons

A custom application could be sabotaged if a user moves around the worksheet at will. You may want to restrict movement within your custom applications or at least provide a message for the user if he clicks on the wrong cell.

One way to provide such a message is to place a large, transparent button over all cells you want to protect. A message can be attached to this button that informs the user to choose one of the proper cells. To create this message, attach a macro that produces a simple text box or alert box to the invisible button.

Use text boxes to display notes

 If you want to display notes to users—when they click a button or select a menu command, for example—try using text boxes. You can easily set up the text boxes to be displayed and hidden when the user clicks the appropriate buttons. Use the HIDE.OBJECT command to perform this function.

Attach the following command to the button or menu command that will display the text box "TEXT1":

```
HIDE.OBJECT("TEXT1",FALSE)
```

Use the command HIDE.OBJECT("TEXT1",TRUE) to hide the text box when the user clicks the other button or command.

Create custom menu commands that toggle

 Like toggle buttons (see the previous tip, "Create toggle buttons"), custom menu commands can toggle from one action to another, helping you to avoid using two menu commands. Examples of toggle menu commands can be found throughout Excel and other Macintosh software.

Creating a toggle menu command requires the use of the RENAME.COMMAND and SET.VALUE macro functions. Following is an example of a macro that produces a toggle menu item.

Notice that the custom menu is called Menu and that the macro begins at cell A1 of the macro sheet:

```
A1:  TOGGLE

A2:  =IF(A2=TRUE,GOTO(A6),GOTO(A2))

A3:  =RENAME.COMMAND(GET.BAR(),"Menu","Toggle On",
"Toggle Off")
```

A4: =SET.VALUE(A6,FALSE)

A5: TOGGLE OFF MENU COMMANDS HERE (change following
line references if more than one line of commands)

A6: =GOTO(A9)

A7: =RENAME.COMMAND(GET.BAR(),"Menu","Toggle Off",
"Toggle On")

A8: =SET.VALUE(A2,FALSE)

A9: TOGGLE ON MENU COMMANDS HERE (Change following
line references if commands take more than one cell)

A10: =RETURN()

Note: The GET.BAR function simply returns the value of the active menu bar. If the custom menu command is on a different menu bar, refer to the appropriate menu bar in place of this command.

Save an invisible worksheet or macro sheet

You may find it tricky to save an invisible worksheet or macro sheet. When you use the Window Hide command to hide the sheet, the Save command no longer recognizes that the sheet exists.

Therefore, to save a hidden worksheet or macro sheet, you must use the Window Hide command, and then quit Excel with the File Quit command. When you are asked if you want to save the changes to the invisible sheet, respond Yes.

Lock a macro sheet in a workbook

You cannot hide a worksheet and add it to a workbook file. Hence, if you have valuable macros that you've included in a workbook file and you don't want anyone to have access to those macros, try using an auto_startup macro that includes the ON.ACTIVATE function to identify when the macro sheet has been activated.

The ON.ACTIVATE macro automatically presents a message informing the user that the macros cannot be viewed and then immediately moves to another page of the workbook. Also, save the macro sheet with a blank area in view.

17

Finding Other Sources of Help

There are many avenues through which you can get additional support for using Microsoft Excel. People and resources are available to help you learn more on your own, to train you, to answer your questions by phone or FAX, and even to develop applications using Excel worksheets and its extensive macro programming language.

Microsoft telephone support

Microsoft maintains telephone support for its products from 6 a.m. to 6 p.m., Pacific Daylight time. The phone numbers listed here usually ask whether you want to hear recorded tips for the most frequently asked questions or whether you want to speak directly to a support person. Microsoft has more than 1,200 employees to support its products.

Some of the technical support numbers you may find useful are listed in the following table:

Description	Telephone Number
Directory of Product Support Numbers	206-454-2030
Sales & Services (upgrades and interim releases)	800-426-9400
Windows 3.1	206-637-7098
Microsoft Excel for Windows	206-635-7070
Microsoft Excel for Macintosh	206-635-7200
Microsoft Word for Windows	206-462-9673
Microsoft Word for Macintosh	206-635-7200
TDD/TT (text telephone for deaf)	206-635-4948

Microsoft automated voice and FAX support

Many of the most frequently asked questions and their answers are available 24 hours a day through Microsoft's automated support system. This system answers the most frequently asked questions on Excel 3 and 4.

You can listen to a voice description of different questions and answers. At the end of each sequence, you are given an opportunity to request a FAX containing the full response. The FAX is usually sent within a few hours.

The automated support service numbers are as follows:

Service	Telephone Number
Windows Excel	206-635-7071
Macintosh Excel	206-635-7081
Windows	206-635-7245

You can navigate through the voice support system using the following touch-tone keys:

Command	Key
Start over	#
Next question	*
Repeat	7
Exit	0

Microsoft on-line for drivers and files

If you need application notes or software drivers other than those notes and drivers on the original installation disks, you can download them directly from Microsoft through their on-line service.

This service also lists telephone support numbers for all Microsoft products. The on-line service requires a modem and communication software. The on-line telephone number is (206) 936-6735.

Communications settings for on-line are:

Baud rate	1200, 2400, 9600
Data Bits	8
Stop Bit	1
Parity	None

These settings are the default settings for your communications program.

Microsoft Excel Wish Line

If you have a feature that you want to see in the next release of Excel or if a feature exists that you feel should be
redesigned, leave your suggestions with the Microsoft
Excel Wish Line. The recorder asks for your suggestion as
well as your name and telephone number so that you can
be contacted if additional information is needed.

Call the Wish Line at (206) 936-9474. You may also send a
FAX to the Excel Wish Line at (206) 93M-SFAX. Address the
FAX to the attention of Microsoft Excel Wish.

CompuServe forums

CompuServe is a public database and bulletin board service that stores business, medical, scientific, and personal
information on many topics. Microsoft maintains numerous databases, bulletin boards (forums), and libraries of
files relating to Excel and other Microsoft products.

If you are already a CompuServe member, you can gain
access to Microsoft forums and libraries by typing one of
the following CompuServe commands after the
CompuServe prompt (!).

CompuServe Command	Description of Location
GO MSOFT	The main menu for all Microsoft services on CompuServe.
GO MSEXCEL	The menu for all forums and libraries related to Excel.
GO MSKB	The menu for the Microsoft Knowl-edge Base. This database contains many of the problems and answers used by Microsoft's telephone support people.
GO MSL	The main menu for the Software Library.

To connect your computer to CompuServe you need to have a CompuServe account and a modem connecting your computer to a telephone. To get an introductory membership to CompuServe, contact CompuServe at (800) 848-8199.

User training

Microsoft certifies training centers that provide introductory- and intermediate-level training on Windows and Excel.

For information about the authorized training center closest to you, call Microsoft sales and services at (800) 426-9400. Skip the numeric phone tree by pressing 0 and asking the operator for the Authorized Training Centers.

Advanced training or corporate consulting and application development

Microsoft maintains a Consultant Relations Program for consultants who develop applications for and support specific Microsoft products. Consultants must take certification exams, submit applications for code review, and submit a list of clients. The highest level of consultant is the Microsoft Consulting Partner.

For corporate consulting or macro-developer training in Excel, call or write Van Buren & Associates at the address below. Van Buren & Associates provides training and custom development for corporations nationwide on Excel and other applications.

Christopher Van Buren is the best-selling author of *Using Excel 4 for the Mac, Special Edition*, published by Que Corporation.

Contact Van Buren & Associates at:

Christopher Van Buren
Van Buren & Associates
P.O. Box 117144
Burlingame, CA 94010
(415) 584-6353

Other books

One of the easiest and least expensive ways to learn more about Excel is through a book. A book is always there when you need it.

Other helpful books on Excel from Que Corporation are:

Using Excel 4 for the Mac, Special Edition
by Christopher Van Buren

This 1,000-page book is the best-selling Macintosh Excel book on the market. It covers Excel basics and continues through creating and customizing charts, using special worksheet features, and developing custom interfaces with macros. It includes hundreds of tips, sample worksheets, and information on every Excel feature.

Que's Big Mac Book, 3rd Edition
by Neil J. Salkind

This 1,000-page book is an A-to-Z introduction to all aspects of Macintosh computing. It provides product comparisons and offers troubleshooting tips and purchasing recommendations.

Excel 4 for the Mac Quick Reference
by Rita Lewis

This 150-page book is a hands-on reference for every command and the new features added to Excel 4 for the Mac.

User groups

One of the largest and most helpful Macintosh user groups is the Berkeley Macintosh User's Group (BMUG). This organization can provide access to support technicians, ready-made Excel templates, public domain software, and more.

Contact them at the following address and phone number for more information.

Phone:
BMUG office line (510) 549-BMUG
Help line (510) 849-HELP

Write:
BMUG
1442A Walnut #62
Berkeley, CA 94709

Index

levels (outlines), 107
line charts, custom system,
149-150
line spacing, 121
linking
formulas between
worksheets, 92-93
legends, 161
reports, 108
worksheets and charts,
151-152
lists, hiding text, 120-121
locking
cells, 79-80
macro sheets, 192

M

Macro Library, 8
macro sheets
saving
as template, 4-5
invisible, 192
templates, 4
workbooks, locking, 192
macros, 169-170
assigning to buttons/
tools, 177-180, 189
capitalization, 170
data entry, 172-173
displaying dialog boxes,
172
locating Startup folder, 6-7
STEP functions, 171
user input, 174-175
Main Chart command (For-
mat menu), 148
margins, 130
MATCH function, 52, 53-54
matching data, 53-54
menus
commands, custom,
191-192
shortcut, displaying, 13-14

merging styles between
worksheets, 62
Microsoft
Excel Wish Line, 198
technical support
FAX, 196-197
drivers/files, 197
telephone support,
195-196
modifying
column width prior to
printing, 130
margins prior to printing,
130
styles, 108
moving
cells, 15, 19-20
express move, 19-20
ranges drag-and-drop, 15
windows, non-active, 166
multiple selections, 185
multiplication, 100-102

N

Name Changer file, 87
named ranges, databases, 134
names
cells, pasting into formulas, 85-86
changing, 86-87
macros, capitalization, 170
ranges, pasting into for-
mulas, 85-86
tools, viewing, 28
naming
cells, 25-26, 106
ranges, 25-26
result cells, 106
sort ranges, 137
navigating
windows, 165
workbooks, 9
NETWORKDAYS function,
52-53

New Window command
(Window menu), 166
Normal style, 65
notes, displaying in text
boxes, 191
NOW( ) function, 48
Number command (Format
menu), 49
Number Format dialog box,
70
numbers
' (apostrophe), 40
" (quotation marks), 40
^ (caret), 40
alignment, 72-73
color, 71-72
converting to text num-
bers, 95-97
formatting, 72, 80
glossary, 45
hiding, 78-79
joining with text, 77
linking with worksheets/
charts, 151-152
rounding, 99
text, converting to values,
39-40
Numbers command (Format
menu), 48
numeric formats
adding text, 71
color, 71-72
custom, 70-71
custom, startup
worksheet, 75
dot leaders/trailers, 74
shortcut keys, 69-70
numeric values
converting to text, 75
verifying, 50

O

OFFSET function, 136-137
opening files, 3, 7
outlines
levels, 107
printing, 123-124
Select as Displayed tool,
107
styles, 108
toolbars, custom, 107

P

page breaks, 127
page numbering, 126
Page Setup command (File
menu), 124, 125
panes (windows) freezing,
166-167, 179
partial styles, 61-62
passwords, 55
Paste command (Edit menu),
83
Paste Function command
(Formula menu), 84
Paste Name command (For-
mula menu), 85
Paste Name dialog box, 86
pasting
arguments, 84
formula bar elements, 83
in dialog boxes, 83
names, calls/ranges, 85-86
pictures, titles, 77
pie charts, 149
playing macros, displaying
dialog boxes, 172
pointer, 15, 18
precedence cells, 89-90
Preferences folder, 3
print area, 129
Print Preview command (File
menu), 130

print settings, 124-125
print titles, 128, 128-129
printing
    adjusting margins, 130
    columns, adjusting width,
        130
    enlarging, 130
    formulas, 90
    outlines, 107, 123-124
    reducing, 130
Protect Document command
    (Options menu), 55
protecting
    cells, 79-80
    worksheets, 54-55, 190

Q-R

quotation marks ("), 40

ranges
    calculated, 183-185
    criteria, *see* criteria ranges
    databases, 134-140
    erasing, 17
    filling, 14
    formats, custom, 49-50
    moving, 15
    names, pasting into for-
        mulas, 85-86
    naming, 25-26
    numeric, verifying, 50
    selecting, 18-19
rebuilding crosstab reports,
    110
recalculating
    crosstab reports, 110
    worksheet portions, 84-85
Record command (Macro
    menu), 172
Record Macro dialog box, 172
recording macros, selecting
    cells, 21
redefining colors, 67

reducing
    printing, 130
    worksheets, 19
references, cell, *see* cell refer-
    ences
relative cell references, 81-82,
    138
reminders, file saving
    (AutoSave), 8
Remove Page Break com-
    mand (Options menu), 127
Remove Print Area command
    (Options menu), 129
Remove Print Titles com-
    mand (Options menu), 129
Rename a Name dialog box,
    86
renaming, 86-87, 161
repeating titles, 128
Replace command (Formula
    menu), 84, 171
reports, 108-109
    creating, 141-143
    extracts, 115
    line spacing, 121
    linking, 108
    summary, 106
    text, hiding, 120-121
    see also Crosstab
        ReportWizard
restoring
    toolbars, 32
    worksheet size, 19
result cells, 106
retrieving results, Crosstab
    ReportWizard, 111-112
right-alignment columns,
    58-59
ROUND function, 99
rounding, 72, 99-100
rows
    deleting, 22-23
    displaying, 63, 116-118

hiding, 63, 116-118
inserting, 22-24
print titles, 128-129
summing, multiple, 93

S

Save As command (File
menu), 4
saving
charts as template, 4-5
files, AutoSave, 8
macro sheets, 4-5, 192
templates in Startup
directory, 4
text strings in glossary, 44
toolbars, 35
worksheets
as template, 4-5
invisible, 192
Scenario Manager, 105-106
scrolling lists, 185
searching, 91-93
security, 55
seed date, 42
segments (pie charts), 149
Select as Displayed tool, 107,
123
Select Current Block tool, 21
Select Special command
(Formula menu), 25, 90
selecting
buttons without running
macro, 178
cells, 21-22, 25
data points (charts),
148-149
graphics without running
macro, 178
large areas, Zoom view, 19
multiple areas, 19
multiple selections, 185
ranges, 18-19
sort range, 137

semicolon (;), 70
sequential dates, 42
serial numbers, 37, 48
series, 41-43
Set Criteria command (Data
menu), 109
Set Database command
(Data menu), 134, 142
Set Print Area command
(Options menu), 124, 129
Set Print Titles command
(Options menu), 128
Set Print Titles dialog box,
128
settings (View Manager),
124-125)
shortcut keys, numeric formats, 69-70
shortcut menus, displaying,
13-14
Sort command (Data menu),
118
Sort dialog box, 133
sorting databases, 118,
133-137
spell-check, 46, 143
Spelling command (Options
menu), 46
splitting windows, 167
Standard toolbar, 31
startup
files, opening automati-
cally, 3
formats, default, 66
worksheets, 5-6
Startup directory, 4
Startup folder, 3, 6-7
STEP function, 171
Step mode, 171
Stop Recorder command
(Macro menu), 173
strings, saving, 44
Style command (Format
menu), 61

workbooks, 8-10, 192
WORKDAY function, 102
Worksheet Auditor com-
  mand (Formula menu), 92
worksheets
  aerial view, 19
  calculating/recalculating,
    84-85
  colors, 66-67
  data entry, group edit, 39
  data transfer, 176
  date and time, displaying,
    48
  default, creating, 5
  formats, transferring,
    74-75
  formatting, multiple, 57-58
  formulas, linking, 92-93
  group edit, 39
  inserting
    cells, 22-24
    columns, 22-24
    glossary entries, 45
    rows, 22-24
  linking to charts, 151-152

protecting, 54-55, 190
recalculating, 84-85
reducing, 19
restoring size, 19
saving
  as template, 4-5
  invisible, 192
startup, 5-6, 75
styles, merging, 62
templates, 4
titles, 128
windows, multiple, 166
Workspace command
  (Options menu), 15

X-Y-Z

zeros
  displaying, 41
  hiding, 77, 78
Zoom command (Window
  menu), 19
Zoom dialog box, 19